Don't Just Bake Cookies

DON'T JUST BAKE COOKIES
A Handbook to Creative Volunteering in the Elementary School

Traci Maxted and Melinda Swezey Tomsic

Illustrated by
Traci Maxted

1990
TEACHER IDEAS PRESS
A Division of
Libraries Unlimited, Inc.
Englewood, Colorado

TEACHER IDEAS PRESS
A Division of Libraries Unlimited, Inc.
P.O. Box 3988
Englewood, Colorado 80155-3988

Library of Congress Cataloging-in-Publication Data

Maxted, Traci.
    Don't just bake cookies : a handbook to creative volunteering in the elementary school / Traci Maxted and Melinda Swezey Tomsic ; illustrated by Traci Maxted.
        xiii, 146 p.   22x28 cm.
    Includes bibliographical references.
    ISBN 0-87287-791-4
    1. Volunteer workers in education--United States--Handbooks, manuals, etc. 2. Creative activities and seat work--Handbooks, manuals, etc. 3. Education, Elementary--United States--Activity programs--Handbooks, manuals, etc. I. Tomsic, Melinda Swezey. II. Title.
LB2844.1.V6M35 1990
372.5--dc20   90-42530
                                                      CIP

Dedication

To our children, Jeffrey and Jennifer Maxted and Jeffrey and Katie Tomsic, without whom we never would have been volunteers, and to our very supportive spouses, Jim and Greg, without whom we never would have conquered our computers.

Contents

**Part 1
Who, Me? Volunteer?**

**Part 2
Parties with a Purpose**

Part 3
The Party's Over But....

Preface

We believe that parents, community members, senior citizens and professional school staff members can and must join hands to become true partners in our children's education. The purpose of this book is to urge volunteers in the elementary school to widen their horizons, to encourage them and their schools' professional staff to see volunteers not just as punch-pourers, cookie bakers, and chauffeurs, but as valuable enrichment facilitators. We hope that volunteers, teachers, and administrators alike will use this book to discover some new, creative avenues for volunteer involvement and to have fun doing it!

The book is divided into three separate sections. Part 1, "Who, Me? Volunteer?", is an overview of voluntarism in the elementary schools; the need for and the profits from volunteers; how and why you as an individual should get involved; how to evaluate, establish, or expand the volunteer programs in your school; your role as a volunteer in the school (your responsibilities and your opportunities); and finally, the possible obstacles you may encounter on your road to becoming a creative volunteer.

Part 2, "Parties with a Purpose," deals with the old tradition of volunteers as party givers but adds a new twist—learning. Instead of writing off classroom parties as free-for-alls or as sugar highs on school time, we present parties that combine fun and learning. In fact, in this book, school parties aren't really parties at all; they are study units with food and games. All of our parties revolve around themes—from Dinosaur Days to Native Americans to Through the Looking Glass—and encourage creative thinking and student involvement. To us, a Mexican party could mean anything from a forty-five minute period spent eating tacos and batting at a piñata to a month-long study unit of our southern neighbors that includes student projects on Mexico's music, geography, arts and culture, religion, games, food, and so on. Volunteers can facilitate this kind of programming and do so, we hasten to add, without an unreasonable time commitment.

The final section, Part 3—"The Party's Over But....", explores other opportunities for volunteer involvement, from small classroom commitments to coordination of all-district programming. By citing examples of programs already in existence, this section illustrates the process of implementing programming in the schools: on-going or special events; curriculum enrichment or fund raisers; programs involving just a few students, an entire classroom, or the whole district. In this section, you will find innovative ideas for implementing programs to emphasize reading, writing, art, math skills, drug awareness, and community service.

The appendixes include lists of addresses of national organizations with information or programs of interest to volunteers, an example of a complete volunteer handbook, and samples of forms and hand-outs helpful for volunteer programming.

Welcome, then, to the wide, wonderful world of volunteering. We guarantee you a better relationship with your school and your child, a deep sense of personal satisfaction, and a clear understanding of the need for more and better parental involvement in our schools. We wish you success—and a few laughs along the way.

Acknowledgments

We'd like to thank the entire staff, student population, and every one of our fellow volunteers at Johnson Elementary School in Cedar Rapids, Iowa, every one of whom has taught us at least one invaluable lesson about being an elementary school volunteer. In addition, we'd like to thank all the volunteers and volunteer coordinators from all over the country who so generously "shared" with us — their booklets, their programs, their philosophies. These helpful folks include Mary Curran, Libby Demerly, Laura Derr, Vicki Filling, Greer Fry, Laura Gesme, Connie Guinnup, Sally Harms, Pam Hunter, Kenneth La Barbera, Eileen Lawson, Anne MacLeod, Jean Meyers, Barb Scott, Jo Stone, and Sharon Wetherall.

We'd especially like to acknowledge Sue Pearson, volunter coordinator for the Cedar Rapids Community Schools, who first recruited and trained us as novice volunteers and whose support and contributions of knowledge and information have been invaluable to the writing of this book. Special thanks, too, go to the world's most personable volunteer coordinator, Karen Carroll, and two of the most volunteer-supportive principals we know: Cynthia Monroe and Steve Chambliss.

Part 1
Who, Me? Volunteer?

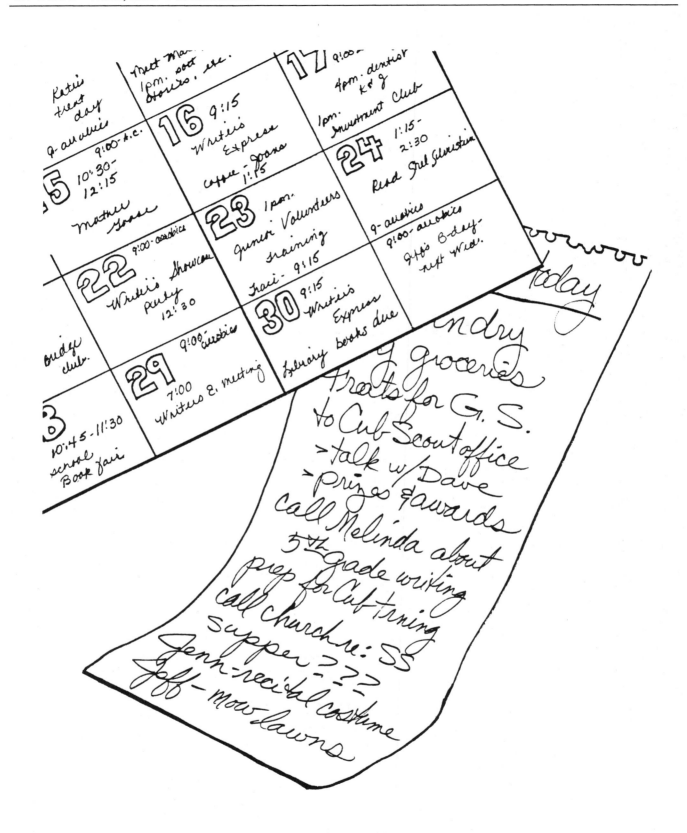

1 Beyond Cookie Baking

Mother Goose and Garfield characters one day, writing conference leader and PTA president the next. So go our lives as just two of the thousands of elementary school volunteers in the country today. As volunteers, we have baked our share of cookies, poured our share of punch, and driven our share of field trips to the apple orchard. (In our case, Traci has baked both of our shares as Melinda hates to bake cookies, especially if she doesn't get to eat them! Melinda has made up for not baking cookies by chaperoning outings to the apple orchard every autumn since 1979.) But we're here to tell you, school volunteering has gone way beyond just baking cookies, pouring punch, and driving on field trips. Take a look at some of the things we've done since we began our careers as elementary school volunteers six years ago. Together, we have donated well over one thousand hours of volunteer work to our school, acting as kindergarten skills helpers (we'll explain what that means in a later chapter), as drivers or chaperons on field trips, as book characters (Garfield and Mother Goose among others) reading aloud to classes, as listeners for beginning readers, as tutors for math and spelling, as skill testing supervisors, and as warm bodies available at short notice whenever and wherever needed. In addition, Traci has served as an officer in the PTA for seven years, including her two-year term as president, has chaired the annual school carnival, and has used her artistic skills on many a poster or cut-out silhouette. Melinda has translated her writing expertise into innovating and coordinating a number of volunteer-supported writing programs. She has coached several dramatic presentations, and on one memorable occasion learned to make corn-husk dolls one day and taught thirty-eight fifth graders to make them the next. Our experiences represent a cross section of the wide variety of volunteering activities going on in our elementary schools today.

In fact, the possibilities for volunteering in the elementary schools are practically endless. Look, for example, at this list of fifty-nine volunteering possibilities as printed in *Effective Involvement of School Volunteers: Handbook for Teachers*, by the National School Volunteer Program.

1. Tell stories to children.
2. Listen to child read.
3. Conduct flash card drills.
4. Provide individual help.
5. Assist in learning centers.
6. Set up learning centers.
7. Help contact parents.
8. Reproduce materials.
9. Work in clinic or library.
10. Check out audiovisual equipment.
11. Practice vocabulary with non-English-speaking students.
12. Make instructional games.
13. Play instructional games.
14. Play games at recess.
15. Assist with visual tests.
16. Prepare visual materials.
17. Develop programmed materials.
18. Grade papers.
19. Prepare bulletin boards.
20. Help with book fairs.
21. Work with underachievers.
22. Reinforce Dolch words.
23. Help select library books.
24. Assist with field trips.

25. Make props for plays.
26. Set up or run bookstore or book exchange.
27. Gather resource materials.
28. Help children learn to type.
29. Teach children to sew, knit.
30. Help children with cooking projects.
31. Check out books from public library.
32. Set up experiments.
33. Take attendance.
34. Collect lunch money.
35. Escort children to bathroom, library, cafeteria.
36. Work on perceptual activities.
37. Make list of library resources.
38. Visit a sick child at home.
39. Work with a handicapped child.
40. Prepare teaching materials.
41. Record grades.
42. Supervise groups taking tests.
43. Discuss careers or hobbies.
44. Show a filmstrip to a group.
45. Help young children with walking on a balance beam, jumping rope, or skipping.
46. Reinforce learning of alphabet.
47. Reinforce recognition of numerals.
48. Drill recognition of colors.
49. Talk to children—be a friend.
50. Help children with motor skills problems.
51. Help children learn a foreign language.
52. Play a musical instrument.
53. Help students who play instruments.
54. Make puppets.
55. Dramatize a story.
56. Help with handwriting practice.
57. Set up "grocery store" to practice math skills.
58. Drill spelling words.
59. Make reading carrels from boxes.

Surely somewhere in that list is a special niche of volunteering that appeals to your interests and abilities. Note the wide variety of opportunities included here and keep in mind this list is in no way all-inclusive; there are definitely more than just fifty-nine ways to volunteer in the elementary school. Note, too, that many of these activities could be interwoven easily into the lives of working parents. Surely, you can see that you, too, can get involved in volunteering.

But why should you? What's in it for you—or your child—or your school? Let us answer that by explaining why we as active, busy women make time for volunteering in our lives.

First, we volunteer for ourselves. We both began volunteering when our boys entered kindergarten. Immediately we saw how valuable it was to actually experience the classroom environment with our children. Suddenly we knew the names of our children's classmates, the personalities of their teachers, the physical layout and the more elusive ambience of the classroom. We observed our children with their peers, in their school environment, relating to their teachers and schoolwork. We were no longer relegated to asking the same, stupid questions like "What did you have for snack?" or "Did you have fun today?"

If one of our Jeffs (we both have boys named Jeff—now teenagers!) complained that so-and-so was being bad today, we knew exactly what he meant. We knew the child, we knew his behavior; possibly we knew of the home environment that may have precipitated such behavior; we were able to respond more empathetically and more knowledgeably to our children than we would have otherwise.

We understood—and sometimes even reminded our children—when it was "Red Day" or "L Day" in kindergarten; when it was a spirit day, and they were supposed to sport school colors; what unit they were working on in social studies; and what project was due Thursday. We could sing along with the school song, recite fingerplays with them, picture the corner of the room in which they snuggled with a teddy bear to read a book, and understand such references as "the sharing table" and the "dictionary station." As much as it was possible, we were partners in their school experience.

We learned, too, that volunteering allowed us the privilege of becoming acquainted with the teachers not just as one of their many classroom parents, but as one of their partners in the educational process. We observed firsthand how the teachers worked in the classroom; we observed them in everyday situations and in everyday emergencies. We were not special guests nor invited observers, rather we were integral parts of the classroom staff. We were a normal fixture to the teachers and the kids, so we saw the real workings of the classroom. By the time of the first conferences in October, we were already on a first-name basis with our children's teachers, and believe us, conferences between working partners are a lot more productive than those between strangers just getting acquainted.

We became familiar with other staff members in the school as well. Seeing us around the halls on a weekly basis, the principal, the secretarial staff, the counselor, the other teachers soon began to think of us as part of the family. We were quickly very comfortable with the school and thus able to express our concerns more casually, more openly, and with a great deal more understanding. Volunteering regularly gives the concerned parent the opportunity to become familiar with school routine as well as the opportunity to express concerns to the administration in a sort of "by-the-way" manner that is less threatening and potentially much more effective. Frankly, we can't imagine not having that kind of relationship with our school. After all, as parents, we are trusting our most precious production to the school's care; we have the right to know how the staff is dealing with that responsibility. To learn that, there is just no substitute for being there.

We have also gained valuable experience, work experience which can be, and frequently is, translated into marketable skills. This may be a direct, obvious relationship. "Volunteer" volunteer coordinators may be hired later as district-employed volunteer coordinators. Classroom volunteers may take jobs as teacher's aides. Teacher-trained volunteers, after their child-rearing years, may reenter the work force as employees of the school at which they volunteered. Or, experience gleaned from school volunteering may make a more subtle contribution to subsequent employment. Volunteering may give young volunteers without previous work experience the confidence to seek employment. Unskilled volunteers get valuable on-the-job training in office procedures. Volunteers with little work experience and, therefore, few references, find professionals willing and able to recommend them for employment. And don't forget people who gained so much from volunteering, they decided to write a book about it!

Of course, for all of us who believe that we are our brothers' keepers, volunteering is a valuable outlet for fulfilling our community responsibility. Is there anything more valuable to any society than its children and is there anyone out there unaware of the atrocities our children are enduring in today's world? Newspaper headlines of child molestations and child abuse are commonplace. Perhaps even more commonplace — and surely a problem we can help correct — is child neglect. Children in all cross sections of society are simply being ignored, lost in the shuffle of parents' struggles to make a living or keep up with the Joneses. Too many children are being left for the schools to nurture. By default, schools have had to take over the role of building positive self-concepts and teaching our youngsters the meaning of doing unto others. You have no idea how important one little pat on the back or encouraging smile can be to today's child. It may be the only such affectionate gesture the child gets that day. Can you stand not to give that? Can you afford not to?

Besides all these wonderfully esoteric, socially responsible reasons for being a volunteer, there is another just as important. School volunteering is fun! If your school is anything like ours, you will be privileged to work in a cheerful, friendly, positive environment with caring, concerned professionals who frequently know some very good jokes. It never hurts any of us, insulated, at-home caretakers or working parents, to expand our horizons socially. Being a school volunteer means meeting lots of new people which frequently translates into making new friends. No doubt you'll make at least one lasting friendship through your school volunteering; more than likely, you'll make many.

We also volunteer because we see it as an extension of our parenting responsibility. We volunteer for our kids' sake. After years of being the most important influence on our children's lives, it seems callous to send our babies to school at age five and expect them to begin cheerfully a life completely independent of our involvement. Being a school volunteer says to your kids that you care — about them, about their school, and about their new lives. Children whose parents volunteer, in whatever capacity, are proud. You can see it in their faces when Mom or Dad or Grandma or Aunt Sophie walks in the room. Volunteering at school also shows your kids that you care about school. If school is important to you, it will be important to them.

Volunteering also gives your children a unique opportunity to see you as more than just their parent. They see you doing a job, relating to other adults, working with other children, being yourself and not just their mom or dad. Even for children of working parents, this may be new—unless you take them with you to work, they don't have an opportunity to see you in this light. Such exposure greatly alters and expands your relationship with your child.

For example, Melinda works as a volunteer in the writing program, leading writing conferences with scores of children, praising and gently prodding them to write their personal best. Occasionally, of course, she has run into the individual child who resists all such efforts to improve his writing, but none more so stubborn as her own son. "No," he'd respond with tears in his eyes, "I don't want to. I like it the way it is."

Melinda shared the problem with his teacher, who surmised that Jeff was confused about Melinda's role in the classroom. He expected her to respond to his writing as his mother, as chief cheerleader and official back-patter. That's what mothers do. She wasn't supposed to act like a teacher. But at school, Melinda wasn't supposed to act like his mother; she was supposed to behave as an educator.

The teacher suggested a group conference including Jeff. That way he could watch Melinda work with his classmates. It worked. As Jeff observed his mother working with his fellow students, praising but also asking for more, for better, Jeff slowly recognized what his mother's role was. He realized at last that his mother was doing a job, that she worked with all the kids the same way. When he saw the improvements in their stories and recognized the fun they were having working on them, then it was O.K. It wasn't Mom correcting him; it was the writing conference leader teaching him and helping him. When it came his turn to read his story and listen to the comments, he responded positively.

Two years later, when Melinda initiated a program to have upper-level grade-schoolers lead writing conferences with first- and second-graders, Jeff was her star participant. In fact, when it came time to train new conference leaders, Melinda enlisted Jeff as her assistant. Watching him confidently and sensitively instruct his classmates in the fine points of conferencing made every hour she had donated worth a thousand. They'd come a long way, together. And so can you and your child!

Lastly, of course, we volunteer because the school needs us. We are all aware of the lack of funds in education. Volunteers fill vital gaps. In the Cedar Rapids school district, volunteers contribute 82,000 hours of work a year, which translates into almost $500,000 of free funding. In Houston, Texas, volunteers donated 1,008,556 work-hours in 1987-1988 or approximately $10,085,560 in cost benefits. Kenneth S. LaBarbera, director of volunteer programs for the Patchogue-Medford Schools in New York, estimates that the 300 volunteers in his district contribute about $100,000 per academic year. In Tulsa, Oklahoma, 4,470 registered volunteers contributed 160,907 hours in 1987-1988. And the list goes on. All over the country volunteers support our nation's schools. We offer much one-on-one attention that teachers are simply unable to give. We sponsor fund-raisers. We teach crafts, direct dramas, organize special events. We supply clerical skills, make field trips possible, brighten classrooms with cutouts and posters teachers are too overworked to produce. We supplement curriculum with tutorial skills. We facilitate small group learning sessions. We enrich classroom curriculum with innovative programs. In short, we make a difference.

RESOURCES

Effective Involvement of School Volunteers: Handbook for Teachers. Alexandria, Va.: National School Volunteer Program, Inc.

McDonald, Nancy, and Zenke, Larry. *A Handbook for School Volunteers.* Tulsa, Okla.: Tulsa Public Schools, Education Service Center, 1988.

School Volunteer Manual. Patchogue, N.Y.: Patchogue-Medford Schools.

VIPS Annual Report. Houston Tex.: Houston Independent School District.

2 O.K., I'm Sold! Now What?

If you're reading this chapter, you must have decided that yes, you, too, would like to make a difference. You'd like to be an elementary school volunteer. Great; we're proud of you and positive that you will never regret this decision.

So how do you get started? Believe us, it's easy. If our research for this book has taught us nothing else, it has taught us that volunteering is going on in schools everywhere around the country. Even if your school doesn't have a very sophisticated program, we'd be willing to bet that some volunteers are being used in your school in some capacity. Even if your school's idea of volunteering is the old traditional "room mother" concept, that's a foot in the door; they're using volunteers. Maybe not well, but they're using them!

In fact, if all you volunteering virgins search your memory banks, you probably remember a note or a newsletter your child brought home or a newspaper notice or PTA announcement requesting volunteers to do some such something at your school: driving or chaperoning a field trip, helping with a special craft project, checking books in the library. Maybe you ignored it because it didn't fit your schedule or your interests. Fine. The point is that many schools are begging for volunteers; all you have to do is offer your warm body and the school will have no problem finding a use for it.

That course, though, can sometimes lead to trouble; it may lead you right into some sort of meaningless drudgery that does not interest you in the least — and that, in turn, will lead you right out the back door. Perhaps a better course is to investigate the possibilities a bit more circumspectly before you offer yourself up at the school's doorstep.

First, ask your kids. Even kindergartners may be able to tell you if Josh's mom comes in once a week to read a story or Jenny's mother teaches them games sometimes; certainly older children can inform you if volunteers are a regular fixture in their classroom. Next ask your friends and neighbors who have children enrolled in your school, especially those with children the same age or a little older than yours. If your school has an active program, you will no doubt quickly encounter at least one volunteer among your acquaintances, and those who are not directly involved will probably know the names of others who are.

This preliminary detective work should give you an overview of the kinds of volunteering activities going on at your school and the person or persons whom you could contact to find out more. More than likely, if your investigation leads to anyone who is very active in volunteering, you may find yourself immediately recruited. Nobody enjoys the thrill of recruiting a new volunteer better than another volunteer. This may just be a good time for you to say yes — no matter what the job is. Getting involved in volunteering through a friend is probably one of the most comfortable ways to begin your volunteer experience. If you decide later the job really isn't for you, you can say that more easily to a friend, and now that you have some experience under your belt, you may be able to pinpoint exactly what it is you'd like to do.

After talking with a number of people, you've learned either that there is a wide variety of volunteer opportunities at your school or that your school's volunteer program is rather limited or even nonexistent. In the latter case, we will speak directly to your predicament in later chapters; but this chapter should give you a clear idea of your role and responsibilities as a school volunteer. If there is some sort of volunteer program in your building, step forward and offer yourself as a willing volunteer. It's time now to talk to the school.

If you have learned the school has a volunteer coordinator as many of them do, you may start there. If your school doesn't have a volunteer coordinator or you don't know the volunteer coordinator, you may feel more comfortable talking first with your child's classroom teacher.

Ask if the teacher would like to use you in the classroom and if so, what kinds of activities would be involved. Try to match your abilities with the teacher's needs and do not be afraid to say no to tasks inappropriate to your skills. If you've never stared a computer monitor in the eye before, you're probably not going to be the best choice to coach kids in keyboarding or programming. If you get along with mechanical objects as well as Melinda does—she holds the midwestern record for breaking a copy machine the most times in the widest variety of ways in one 40-minute period—you're probably not going to enjoy spending your morning doing battle with the mimeographing machine.

On the other hand, be open, too. Don't immediately say "I can't." Isn't that what you tell your kids? "Don't give up before you try!" "You never know what you're good at until you try everything!" Wise words, Mom and Dad, so practice what you preach. Maybe you haven't worked on a computer before, but training might be offered through the school that could teach you to be as competent at the keyboard as your eight-year-old. You *can* teach an old dog new tricks. Whatever your writing, reading, math skills are, you probably do know more about these basics than the average ten-year-old. Believe us, it doesn't take a college degree to read a spelling list to a third-grader or listen to a proud first-grader stumble through reading a first book. It just takes someone who cares to take the time. And every minute you offer in tasks such as these frees the expert, the teacher, to concentrate on higher-level teaching activities.

Be specific. Specify exactly how much time you will be willing to give, on what days, and what time of day. Make sure both you and the teacher are clear about what time and what days you'll be in and exactly what you'll be doing when you are there. Nothing is more discouraging to a volunteer than to take the time to come to school, only to find nothing to do. Nor do teachers appreciate planning lessons around the help of volunteers who don't appear when they are scheduled!

Be honest. If you're unsure about what you're being asked to do, speak up. If you're in over your head, ask for help. If you come to the point where, for whatever reasons, you just can't do it anymore, say so.

Most of all never, never let yourself be under-used. Don't let there be any more cases like that of Kathy, a certified, experienced teacher and a very active community volunteer who has served on boards managing million-dollar budgets. When her daughter entered a new school, Kathy offered that building two hours a week of her valuable time. When she arrived to volunteer the first day, she was led to a back office where she spent two hours filing emergency cards. Kathy never went back. That school lost a valuable resource by failing to recognize and utilize one woman's unique skills. Rather emulate Joan, a woman who was not interested in tutoring children in any capacity but wished to support her school's volunteer writing program. A skilled typist, she conquered her fear of computers and now works a word processor several hours a week making publishable the scrawled masterpieces of hundreds of children.

Don't think that because you're employed you can't get involved in volunteering: Many meaningful volunteer opportunities can be worked around work schedules. Working parents can act as organizers, making phone calls in the evening to schedule guest speakers, field trips, and so on. They can sit in on planning sessions for school events and help with preparations outside of working hours. They can record stories onto tapes to be played by beginning readers at school. They can type manuscripts in their spare time. They can take a lunch hour and offer that hour in volunteer time at school. They can take a personal day to spend a few hours at school. Working parents: Be open, be creative, and read on. Do not use your job as an excuse not to get involved; it could be a decision you'd live to regret.

Not only should good volunteers match their skills with their activities; they must also be well aware of their responsibilities as volunteers. Volunteer handbooks from schools around the country have shown us that a number of basic rules are inherent in all schools. Find out if your school has written up a set of specific guidelines for volunteers, and if so, make yourself familiar with it.

If your school has no such document, offer to help get one written. We have studied many of them from school districts all over the country. Dozens are out there already, beautifully written by volunteers in other communities. As Barbara Carter and Gloria Dapper point out in *School Volunteers: What They Do and How They Do It*: "Creativity isn't the only hallmark of the volunteer. We've also discovered a universal tendency toward larceny. Begging, borrowing, and stealing ideas from each other's programs has been a prime factor in the phenomenal growth of the volunteer movement."

We think it heartwarming to discover how willing volunteers and volunteer coordinators across the country are to share their ideas. In that spirit, we include in the appendix the Volunteer's Handbook for the Cedar Rapids School District. It is not unique; in fact, it, like many others, borrows heavily from its fellow publications in other districts. It is, however, short, simple, to the point, easy to read, and pleasant to look at; all important factors in compiling such a book. Look it over. (Note the discussion at the end on insurance coverage; such important information should always be included in a volunteer guide. Check with your school district and/or state legislator to learn the specifics of your state laws.) In addition, check our bibliography at the end of the book for addresses of other district volunteers who may be willing to share information with you.

You say you can't write, or that you couldn't possibly put together such a booklet? Can you type? Run a word processor? Make phone calls? Organize a committee? All of these are skills necessary for producing a school booklet. Surely you can assist in one of these ways and know others who might be willing to help with the rest. You're on your way!

After reading the Cedar Rapids booklet, you should have a pretty clear idea of the responsibilities of the school volunteer. You should have a good idea of what school administrators expect from their volunteers and what school volunteers can expect from their experience. We'd like to reiterate a few important points.

Generally speaking, all schools expect their volunteers to view their commitment professionally. A responsible employee does not ignore a business meeting or fail to show up for work on a whim; likewise, a responsible volunteer does not let down her school. If you cannot fulfill a commitment, call the school and let the staff know as far in advance as possible. Remember that whatever it is you're scheduled to do, the teacher is counting on you and has included you in the daily lesson plan. If you simply don't show or notify the teacher just ten minutes beforehand, you could really interfere with instructional activities.

Of course, most teachers are parents, just as are most volunteers, so they'll understand things like Ashley upchucking all over your shoes on your way out the door. Some absences just cannot be anticipated. Just ask Ashley to try not to make a habit of such surprises!

In addition, most schools expect volunteers to dress appropriately and to behave professionally in the building. We're not talking white gloves and curtsies here; we're just talking common sense. If you're scheduled to assist in throwing clay pots, your worst-looking sweatshirt and holey jeans might be suitable attire; for any other school activity, they probably would not be. Children in schools are expected to walk quietly and calmly through the hallways and not to greet friends in loud voices, chew gum, use foul language, and so on. Certainly we can expect the same modes of courteous behavior in our visiting adults. Your school may have additional regulations regarding such activities as drinking and eating in work areas, designated smoking areas, and the like. Ask your teacher, volunteer coordinator, or other school worker about these.

By virtue of your volunteering involvement, you become a trusted member of that school staff, privy to information that, as fellow professionals, you will be expected to consider confidential. You may see your neighbors' children's grades; you may observe instances of their inappropriate behavior; you may become aware of their learning disabilities, their emotional stresses, their health problems, their classroom social status, their academic achievement. None of this is fodder for supermarket gossip or the telephone grapevine. That pompous little brat of hoity-toity Janette Marshall down the street may just be dumb as a post and a constant source of exasperation to his teacher, but you'll just have to relish these satisfying tidbits of information all by yourself. On the other hand, if you want to share your concern over little Samantha who seems uncharacteristically silent and sullen, do so—with the teacher, and perhaps the counselor and the principal. But leave it at that. Don't go home and share your concern with your spouse at the dinner table even though your eight-year-old seems completely absorbed in "Nik Rocks" on television. Children are only deaf and mute when asked to clean their rooms or change their underwear; mention in a whisper, four rooms away, something about one of their classmates, and they will hear every word you say!

Occasionally volunteers at school, just as parents at home or any other person on the job, will be faced with emergency situations. The child you're teaching to skip may twist his ankle or fall and crack his wrist bone. A first-grader intent on concentration may just bite off his pencil eraser and choke on it. A child in writing group may unexpectedly fall into diabetic shock. What would you do?

Before such emergencies occur, prepare yourself by recognizing that they could happen to you. Be familiar with emergency first aid techniques like the Heimlich maneuver. Ask the teacher if your charges have any medical conditions like diabetes or epilepsy, of which you should be aware. Know who deals with medical matters—the school nurse, the health secretary—and where that office is. When and if an emergency occurs, stay calm. Take whatever immediate action is necessary and quickly notify the appropriate staff member. Do *not* attempt to treat the child beyond immediate lifesaving measures.

Understand what is not your responsibility. Generally, volunteers do not discipline or evaluate students. Those are teacher responsibilities. Naturally, if you are working with a small group of children or an individual child outside the classroom, you are expected to keep order in your group and keep the children on task. However, if real problems occur, take the offending child back to the classroom, and let the teacher deal with the child.

Volunteers do not initiate instruction. If you are an expert flutist, say, or mathematician, or poet, you may be asked to come share your expertise with a class, even teach a workshop. In these instances you will be offering instruction, but it is enrichment not curriculum. You may even "initiate" these activities by coming up with the suggestion, but all such activities are subject to the approval of school staff.

You are not responsible for taking social issues into your own hands. Should you suspect child abuse or sexual abuse in the experience of one of the children with whom you are working, tell the teacher. It is the teacher's responsibility, legal and ethical, to deal with such situations, with the training, expertise, and the experience to make professional evaluations of such suspicions. Should you see further evidence of such problems, speak to the teacher again. If he or she seems not to put credence in your suspicions, and you are really concerned or you have outside information which the teacher ignores, go to the principal and/or the counselor. We think it highly unlikely in today's world that even going beyond the teacher would be necessary, but if in an extreme case everyone at the school seems to be ignoring a situation and you have unquestionable evidence of serious abuse, then you may consider calling in governmental authorities. Let us stress that we are highly skeptical that such a step should ever have to be taken by a volunteer, and would only advise doing so in cases where you sincerely believe a life is being threatened.

Let a smile be your umbrella. Emergencies such as the ones discussed above are quite rare, but minor upsets are the norm in any elementary school. Somebody tosses his or her cookies in the hallway at least once a month. Fifth-grade boys find something to tussle about every recess. Once a week somebody humiliates himself or herself by wetting their pants. Don't be surprised when somebody takes Jason's coat and hides it in Julie's locker for a joke and Jason wants to call in SWAT detectives to find the culprit or when Christopher begins hyperventilating because Jonathan made fun of his cursive or when both the copy machine and the mimeo die of natural causes within a half hour so that there are no worksheets for the second grade. To quote a current profound philosophy, "Don't worry; be happy." See the humor in these situations. More important, if you can help the participants in these daily tragedies see the humor in their predicaments, you've done your day's work as a volunteer.

RESOURCES

ABC's, A Handbook for Educational Volunteers. Washington Technical Institute, 400 Connecticut Ave., NW, Washington, D.C., 20068.

Bennet, Linda Leveque. *Volunteers in the School Media Center.* Englewood, Colo.: Libraries Unlimited, 1984.

Carter, Barbara, and Dapper, Gloria. *School Volunteers: What They Do and How They Do It.* New York: Citation Press, 1972.

Feeney, Helen M., and Stenzel, Anne K. *Volunteer Training and Development: A Manual for Community Groups.* Seabury Press, 1968.

VIPS, Volunteers in Public Schools. Milwaukee, Wis.: Milwaukee Public Schools.

Volunteer Handbook. Cedar Rapids, Iowa: Cedar Rapids Community Schools.

Volunteer Handbook. Duval, Fla.: Duval County Schools.

Working Together, District Eleven School Volunteer Handbook. Colorado Springs, Colo.

3 Never Too Proud to Beg

Establishing a Volunteer Program in Your School

What happens if you ask your children, your friends, your neighbors about the volunteer program at your school, and you come up with nothing but blank stares, shrugged shoulders, and/or a contemptuous snort? It sounds as if the volunteer program at your school might be a little lacking.

"Volunteers!?" the school secretary replies to your telephone inquiry in a perfect Roseanne Barr whine. "Hey, Dodie," she screeches to her office mate. "Some crackpot on the phone wants to know about our volunteer program. Lah Dee Dah. Maybe she'd like to volunteer to fix that running toilet in the boy's john." The line fills with witchlike cackling, then clicks and goes dead.

If this scenario in any way resembles your experience, it's safe to say that voluntarism is not a high priority in your area. But, no matter how discouraging things seem, don't give up. All is not hopeless; you just need to find alternate routes to success.

Our first suggestion is to talk to your child's classroom teacher. Arrange a meeting at a time and place convenient to both of you when and where you will not be interrupted by children or other staff members. Meet privately in the teacher's room or office before or after school hours; not in a community workroom, office, or lounge. You might consider inviting the teacher to your house for after-school tea or out to lunch on Saturday as long as such an invitation doesn't hint of sneaking behind administrators' backs. Try to circumvent administrative resistance without compromising the teacher's professional position.

Start the meeting off warmly by presenting the teacher with a plant or special baked good as a thank-you gift for general hard work or for a particular way in which the teacher helped your child or the class. Or you might have happened on a special book—a finely illustrated collection of poetry, or a resource volume pertinent to the class's current studies, or a clever collection of reward stickers—that might be nice for the teacher to use in the classroom. The point is not out-and-out bribery. You just want to be considered a supportive influence and partner in the educational process. Approaching teachers and administrative staff members with respect and understanding builds successful working relationships.

At your parent-teacher meeting, gently lead into a discussion of your interest in volunteering in the classroom. If the teacher responds in the traditional bake-cookies, pour-punch mode, don't immediately reject those suggestions. Be willing to follow the lead of your teacher. Be agreeable. Be more than happy to assist in traditional ways. That certainly gets your foot in the door. But don't leave it at that.

Before the meeting you should have done your homework, and have some clear ideas about what you'd like to do. You need to have evaluated your special skills and interests and the amount of time per week you are willing and able to donate easily. (Always underestimate this at the beginning!) Compare these with the kinds of needs you have observed or are aware of in your child's classroom.

These needs may be specific. You've noticed that your third-grader does little or no writing, your fourth-grader seems bored with math, your kindergartner hasn't had any field trips, or you may have read in the local paper that district goals include emphasis on language skills or the national news has reported a national deficiency in geography. If you have expertise in any of these areas, you may be just the person to provide some needed enrichment in one of these areas.

If you need help determining such needs, do some simple research. Go to the district school board meetings. Inquire about published policy reports which would include lists of district goals and requirements. Talk to friends and neighbors and listen to their views about their schools. Read the local newspaper's education section. Be an informed observer.

And, of course, read this book for specific ideas about enriching volunteering possibilities. Pay special attention to the "How to Party" chapters as they offer creative approaches to traditional room mother functions and chapter 12 which deals with specific classroom activities. We believe these are the good ways to open the closed doors of elementary schools devoid of volunteer programs.

When presenting your ideas to your teacher, do so in a totally nonthreatening manner. You are not criticizing the school because of a deficiency; you are just wondering if it's not possible to improve on an already perfectly acceptable program and offering yourself as a possible new enrichment resource.

In these early discussions, keep your ideas small. Don't draw up a proposal for an elaborate, high-minded enrichment unit for which you take total responsibility. That kind of thing can scare off even the most accepting of teachers and daunt even the most experienced volunteer. Start small and see the usefulness in even the seemingly insignificant activities.

Take note of a story told to us by Elaine Fox, a kindergarten teacher. Years ago before volunteers were much a part of her classroom experience, Mrs. Fox had a mother offer to come to the classroom one morning a week and work with small groups of children. Happy to have the help and eager to be able to separate the class into small groups and give each child more individual attention, Mrs. Fox agreed. She suggested her volunteer come in and play the board game Candyland with two or three children at a time.

What educational value is there in Candyland, you may ask. First of all, twirling the spinner to take a turn and grasping and moving the plastic players around the board develop hand-eye coordination and fine motor skills. Moving players around the board demands color recognition and an understanding of the concepts of forward and backward. Counting is easily introduced into the action though not necessarily to the game itself. In addition, following the rules of any board game teaches the social skills of taking turns, sharing the focus of attention, delayed gratification, setting up and working toward a goal, patience, perseverance, and good sportsmanship. We'll bet you never saw that much significance in a simple game of Candyland.

Naturally the same lessons plus more advanced ones in logic and strategy can be learned by older children playing more difficult board games such as backgammon, parcheesi, and even chess. Before you leap at the seemingly easy and enjoyable volunteer opportunity of going to school and playing games, remember you must match your personality as well as your skills to your volunteer commitments. Some of the longest hours of Melinda's life were spent playing tortuously drawn-out games of parcheesi with some very persistent third-graders to whom the concept of "get it done fast, get it done clean" meant nothing. If you, like Melinda, tend toward fantasies of strangling any person taking more than thirteen seconds for a turn at Scrabble, perhaps this volunteer opportunity is not for you. However, if you have a more placid soul and patient heart, you might really enjoy this.

Note that we suggest approaching your classroom teacher first because we assume that the two of you already have at least a nodding acquaintance and because we assume if a building has no existing volunteer program at all, it's probably because the principal is resistant to it. This is not always a fair assumption, of course. Maybe there's no such program because nobody has suggested one to the principal before; maybe you should be the first. No harm in trying, especially if you approach the principal as we suggested you approach the teacher. It may be, too, that your teacher will suggest a meeting with both you and the principal. That also would seem a pretty good idea. If you hit a blank wall with either or both of them, read on—and also read chapter 5!

Alternately, you may begin your volunteer experience through the PTA. Literally every school has some sort of parent-teacher organization or parent support group in existence; a good first step to becoming an active volunteer is to attend one of their meetings. Listen carefully to the discussions and when appropriate ask questions. If the concerns tend toward raising funds for new playground equipment and/or preparing a covered dish for the teacher appreciation luncheon, so be it. These are certainly valid, useful functions of concerned parents. Witness the testimony of Anne MacLeod, Newport News, Virginia, parent of a child who attended private elementary school.

I am not crazy about committee work, but I was on one committee that I thought was effective. Parents considered changes in class size a breach of faith. Our protest did some good. So committees can help and volunteers can not only enrich, but also change policy when necessary.

As a teacher in the public school system, Ms. MacLeod added that she felt parents could be more effective than teachers and even teachers' unions in protesting such administrative policies as class size.

While we work toward broadening the views of parents and teachers to see volunteering in terms of creative classroom enrichment, we must work within the system and try to avoid ruffling feathers. Do not

look down your nose at the traditional mind-set of parents' groups who see their roles as collecting dues, debating colors of paper products at the teacher appreciation luncheon, and/or organizing committees for a bake sale. Appreciate that attending a parents' meeting of any kind allows you the opportunity to make contact with an established network of interested, caring parents. Often, too, the PTA or other parents' group will be the source of funds for any start-up and maintenance costs of volunteering programs.

During the meeting or afterward in private conversation as you introduce yourself to organization officers, inquire about the volunteer programs available. Often you will find yourself being recruited for this or that committee. Unless you find the prospect totally beyond your ken, accept.

Working hard at whatever committee work is offered you proves you to be a committed, concerned member of the school community. As you build such a reputation, you build a foundation for positive response to your future suggestions. You will become familiar with needs in the building and can therefore make more pertinent volunteer suggestions in a nonthreatening context.

There are other avenues to open volunteering in buildings when voluntarism is limited or nonexistent. Try speaking to the librarian about helping out there an hour a week—helping kids check out books, shelving books, or doing paperwork. Offer yourself as a resource for a kindergarten story hour when you could read aloud to groups of children. Offer to work in the office during the secretary's lunch hour or to help with filing, copying, typing—whatever suits your time and skills. The office and the library or instructional materials center (IMC) are usually two places you can establish yourself as a volunteer without stepping on any toes. Remember to keep your commitments small at first.

Once you've gotten your feet wet either through the committee work or by volunteering in your child's classroom or building for a period of time, start spreading the word and trying to expand the volunteer horizons. Talk to your friends, neighbors, and school staff about what a positive experience your volunteering has been or what a positive impact more creative volunteering might have on the school. Feel out members of the community and members of the staff about their reactions to volunteers in the building.

If you're already volunteering in the classroom, touch base frequently with your teacher about how he or she feels about your presence. Stop by after school—consult only during noninstructional time—and make sure that the teacher is satisfied with your contribution. Discuss any questions or problems you had. Try to keep communications open and honest at all times.

Keeping up good, clear communications with your teacher makes for a successful volunteer experience in more ways than one. Communication allows both of you to be comfortable with your role and keeps your voluntarism moving in the right direction. It also ensures that the teacher is satisfied with your work, and satisfied teachers are our best advertisements. If you're really an asset to the classroom, the teacher will carry the good news to the teachers' lounge, the principal's office, and staff meetings. In fact, we hope that your classroom teacher comes to feel as strongly about you as Terry Firth, author of *Secrets Parents Should Know about Public Schools*, felt about Linda.

She was an answer to my students' needs and my dreams.... She asked relevant questions relating to the tasks I outlined for students.... She tested students, assisted them with assignments, and taught them many things about other cultures.... She respected cultural differences and never caused a child to feel unacceptable.... She chose [noninstructional] times to specifically compliment me about students' progress, my instructional methods, and overall program.... In addition to her emotional support and caring, she brought me occasional gifts to say she enjoyed working with me.... Several of my students jumped ahead two or three grade levels.... These students' educational experiences were dramatically improved because of dear, dear Linda.

Such revelations from a teacher will elicit curiosity from coworkers. Note the questions Ms. Firth was showered with about Linda.

Despite her obvious contributions to the students' overall progress, however, many of the other teachers' comments were primarily expressions of fear, discomfort, and distrust, such as: "Why don't you put her in the hall with a child?" "Doesn't it take up too much of your time showing her what needs to be done?" "Doesn't she get in your way?" "Doesn't she waste your time talking about things that have nothing to do with your work?" "Are you worried that she'll talk about you?" Or they made excuses for not using volunteer help such as: "I would use a volunteer but I just can't find the time to plan for one." "Volunteers always gossip about the things that happen in class." "It's just more trouble than it's worth."

A classroom teacher who can respond positively to concerns such as these will be doing great public relations work for future volunteers, laying the groundwork for future volunteer opportunities.

In the meantime, we advise you to keep a pretty low profile during the first few weeks of your volunteer experience. Smile and be friendly to everyone, but let your teacher take the lead in introducing you to other staff members and showing you the ropes. Don't just waltz into the teacher's lounge or take over the copy machine without clearing it first with your teacher.

Do check in at the main office each time you arrive and leave and wear a name tag. Both are excellent and necessary security measures—elementary schools these days need to keep close tabs on who is in the building—and the name tag is a thoughtful courtesy to staff members and children who may forget your name from one week to the next. These are also subtle, nonthreatening ways to make staff, parents, and students aware of your presence.

As the time passes keep your volunteer presence on the minds of other staff members by making yourself and your contributions a little more visible. Now don't go strutting off bragging to all and sundry how wonderful you are. Quietly make yourself obvious. Find a corner of the teachers' lounge or workroom—if volunteers are welcome there—to cut out letters or do paperwork. Volunteer to decorate the main bulletin board in the main hallway and do something that really catches everyone's attention. Meet with children in the IMC or hallway where others can observe you working together. Stop by the principal's office to express thanks for the opportunity to work in the building. Talk to your friends and neighbors—without breaking any confidences, of course. Don't lord it over them about how involved you are or insinuate that they are bad parents for not thinking of volunteering first, just talk about your volunteering in a manner that whets their appetites to share similar experiences.

And keeping the title of this chapter in mind, don't be above a little well-meant bribery. Bring gifts. Bake up some muffins for the office staffers who taught you how to work the mimeo. Put a potted plant on the librarian's desk as a thank-you for helping you find a book you needed. Cut some daffodils out of your garden and bring a bouquet just to brighten up the teacher's desk and day.

Be thoughtful. Write a thank-you note to the principal for allowing you the opportunity to share in your child's educational experience. Inquire about staff members' families. Make yourself helpful in unassigned ways—without stepping over your bounds. If you are in the office when three lines on the phone are ringing, a child is about to vomit, and an impatient parent is waiting to ask a question, and there is one secretary on duty, don't just stand there! Answer the phone. If you have fifteen minutes free before your next task, drop by the office, the IMC, or the workroom and offer your services for that time period.

If you are not already working in the building, make your presence and face known. Stop by the school and speak directly to the principal about a question or concern rather than just calling on the phone. When you have occasion to be at the building, have a friendly word and smile for everyone. Ask for advice from any staff person who might be deemed expert in an area. Ask the P.E. teacher about the advisability of your third-grader participating in Little League. Consult with the art teacher about a good drawing book to buy Jennifer for Christmas. Share a fascinating article on sibling rivalry with the counselor. Do this if you are already in a classroom as well. Everybody loves to be treated like an expert and looked to for advice. When you treat staff members with respect for their professional status, you build a positive, sharing relationship which will help belay any future feelings of your trying to infringe on their territory.

Your sincere gestures of goodwill and thoughtfulness will go a long way toward establishing you as a welcome addition to the school family, and lay the groundwork for a similar positive response to other future volunteers. In the words of *Bye, Bye, Birdie*, though, "You gotta be sincere!" If your gestures are nothing more than that, empty gestures; if your kindnesses fail to cover your deep-seated contempt for those whom you are buttering up, you'll do a great deal more damage than if you had done nothing at all. Even in the case of severe personality conflicts, it is possible to offer praise, thanks, and even flowers sincerely if you are making the effort out of concern for the children. You may not respect the person—but you may respect the person's authority, learning, and/or intentions. If you look at the whole situation as a battle in which you and the school staff are allies against an enemy of boring, mediocre education, it should work. However bad some teachers or administrators may be, they are not doing poorly by the children intentionally. In most cases, you will discover that the more you work with educational professionals, the more respect and understanding you will gain, and the more sincere any gesture of appreciation will become.

After a few months of gaining the confidence of the staff and getting to know the building routine and expectations of the administration and staff, it may be appropriate to go public. Attend a PTA meeting and make a formal report either on your volunteer experiences or on the possibilities you see for volunteer involvement. Recommend opportunities you see for more parents to become involved. Propose that a committee be set up to lay out specific plans or offer to act as volunteer liaison between staff and PTA.

Remember that a volunteer program must always be fully supported by the school staff. The pivotal member of that support system, of course, is the principal. Without a supportive principal, there will not be a volunteer program—even if there has been one in the past. Witness the experience of one concerned parent in the St. Louis area who through her publication of a school newsletter offered a writing program and an outlet for student writers in her elementary school. The program went well for a number of years until her supportive principal moved. The incoming principal, finding the role she had assumed to be too powerful and too threatening, summarily terminated the program.

We include this tale as a way of warning. Such unexpected sudden ambushes can hit anywhere, anytime. Our only defense is to be aware of how tentative a volunteer's position within the system is. Obviously, voluntarism, like any other pursuit, is not a path without roadblocks. For more advice on how to deal with administrative resistance, see chapter 5. Our point is, though, that one must never proceed without clear communication with and the complete cooperation of the principal.

So far, as we have laid out your route, you as the premier volunteer are taking on the majority—if not all—of the responsibility for establishing a volunteer program. This may seem to be an overwhelming commitment, at first, but the solution is the first rule of good volunteering—recruit, recruit, recruit.

If you can, recruit an ally, a very good friend just as commited to the concept of creative volunteering in the school as you are to help carry the load of coordinating the early planning. As you go more and more public, never turn down an offer of help from anyone. Learn to delegate.

Traci tells of her two-year stint as PTA president:

> Everyone always went out of their way to try not to load me down with the trivial stuff. They were all too familiar with PTA presidents who had burned out because of that. Trouble was, I

was already good at delegating. Most of my "work" consisted of calling people on a regular basis and asking, "How are you doing? Is it going all right? Don't forget the meeting." Except for one or two minor tasks that no one else wanted, I did less those two years than in any others!"

Words to live by. You can't do it all, and with a little careful delegating, you might not even have to try. It's hard at first to let go. Everybody has a different style of getting things done. Still, you've got to let others do their share; the way they get it done may be different than the way you'd do it, but that doesn't make it wrong; that just makes it different! And remember not to try to second-guess everyone. You never know who's going to say yes until you ask them!

If you really care passionately about creating a volunteer program, you may find yourself, particularly in the early stages of setting up a program, taking on a very heavy load. Be careful of that. A successful volunteer program is one that has its feet widely planted across the entire cross-section of the school population and surrounding community. Avoid the pitfall of the volunteer program as a closed society, populated by a close-knit group of friends all from the same two-block area. That's a pretty foreboding fortress to an outsider.

Such practices as scheduling meetings only during school hours, limiting volunteer programs to those requiring high-level thinking skills, not publicizing meetings and volunteer opportunities, and always calling on the same limited lists of people when help is needed all close doors in the faces of willing volunteers. Expand your horizons. Seek names of helpful folks from all the teachers and administrators in your building. And don't leave out the community at large. Talk to senior citizen groups, church guilds, special interest organizations, and community and business leaders—all rich resources.

Perhaps we can also relieve some of the anxieties we've set loose by reminding you that all successful volunteer programs start small. No multifaceted, ultra-sophisticated, full-blown volunteer program ever just exploded full-functioning onto the scene. Volunteer programs *evolve*—slowly. They all began with just one caring parent like you interested in doing a little something for the school, and grew slowly over the year. This book offers you the opportunity to study how some great oaks from little acorns grew; to see the possibilities and be able to set some long-term goals—and to avoid many of the pitfalls that past pioneering volunteers had to find for themselves, one rotten experience after another.

But, right now, you need to be concerned only with the little acorns and how to plant them in rich, fertile soil so that they may sprout and grow stronger each year, with or without your guidance and support. Your goal should be to know that the volunteer seeds you are sowing now will be reaped not only by you and your children, but by your next-door neighbors and their newborn, and by your unmarried nieces and nephews and their children, and yes, perhaps by your children and your grandchildren.

RESOURCES

Carter, Barbara, and Dapper, Gloria. *Organizing School Volunteers.* New York: Citation Press, 1972.

Firth, Terry. *Secrets Parents Should Know about Public Schools.* New York: Simon and Schuster, 1985.

MacLeod, Anne (volunteer, Newport News, Va.). Personal communication, December 1988.

4 A Person Who Won't Hear No!

The Role of the Volunteer Coordinator

There are varying levels of volunteer coordinator roles in our schools and many titles for these positions. In your area, people who coordinate volunteer efforts may be called enrichment coordinators, community liaisons, resource coordinators, PTA president, volunteer chairpeople, a combination of the above, or something else entirely. If you are pioneering such a position in your school and are working with a very resistant staff, couching your role in a somewhat obscure title like *community liaison* might be a diplomatic tactic, but to paraphrase Shakespeare, "a volunteer coordinator by any other name would work as well."

Naturally, the extent of the responsibility of a volunteer coordinator depends directly upon the scope of the volunteer programs in that building. Few schools are lucky enough to find funding to pay a full- or part-time volunteer coordinator (and even then these dedicated people do not get paid nearly what they're worth). In most cases, building volunteer coordinators are volunteers themselves, many of whom function under the direction of district-employed volunteer coordinators. Though the job descriptions of those whom we are describing as *district* volunteer coordinators may include a wide variety of other community responsibilities, most districts do employ someone whose job it is to supervise and coordinate volunteer efforts in individual buildings. We can only hope that the trend will be to focus more directly on the volunteer component and that attitude will trickle down so that more and more individual buildings can profit from the luxury of having a full-time volunteer coordinator, who, because of education and experience, is considered a fellow professional member of the elementary school community.

For our purposes we will label anyone a volunteer coordinator from the moment that volunteer expands his or her role from just a single volunteer to a volunteer advocate and recruiter. At that moment, a volunteer becomes in one sense or another, a volunteer coordinator. No need for panic! Remember what we said about starting small; this is not a full-time job—yet!

Your first lesson as volunteer coordinator is planning. Sit down with your principal and, if you can find them, a couple of other interested parents whom you trust and know are bright, intelligent, creative people. (We don't mean by "if you can find them" that there aren't a lot of bright people out there, it's just that they're usually busy people and frequently hard to find available!) Together, you should have a team of educators—including you, for all good parents are educators—who can work profitably together to set out some goals for a volunteering program, some specific formats for carrying out those goals, and the necessary human and other resources for implementing those programs.

We were recently in just such a process when we were asked by the PTA president of an area middle school to write up a proposal for devising a writing program there. This was a school with a past history of very limited volunteer involvement. The writing program was to be their first, tentative step toward including volunteers in the classroom. This is the time to make very clear the goals of such a program and the responsibilities of volunteers involved.

Since we have experience in coordinating volunteer-supported writing programs, and since those soliciting the proposal knew that, the actual meeting of minds to set up goals was sidestepped a bit: we substituted a phone call for that step. Within a week of the request, we sent a written proposal to the PTA president, which included ten goals that could be achieved by establishing a volunteer writing program of some kind at that school. Next, three specific program suggestions were outlined, explaining the format of each, the kind of volunteer commitments each would require, the estimated costs of establishing and maintaining such a program, and the goals that would be met by each program. Since these analyses were based on our experience in coordinating similar programs at the elementary level and Melinda's experience and training in teaching writing to middle-school children, the proposal gained a certain quantity of expertise and credibility.

The next step in the process will be for the PTA president, the principal of the building, the language arts teachers, and program coordinators to sit down together and discuss the possibilities. That meeting may result in choosing one of the suggested programs as suggested, in choosing a program with certain specific revisions, or in the evolution of an entirely new program incorporating aspects of each of several programs.

Never, never let your ideas be cast in iron no matter how successful they've been in the past or in other buildings. And never expect to retain ownership of a program. All volunteer programs should be evolutionary—evolving and expanding as conditions demand. Your commitment to such a program probably lasts only as long as your child is in that building or that grade level. A successful program continues much longer than that.

The next step in the process of establishing the writing program will be to begin the process of recruiting interested, qualified parents to staff the program. They, then, can move on to outlining specific guidelines for the program, setting up timetables for implementing the program, and educating the students, staff members, and parents about the program.

Once you have established specific goals and objectives for your volunteering program, it is time to learn the most effective tool in volunteer coordinating—how to beg.

There is a certain persuasive push, more pleasant than a whine, more powerful than a plea, subtler than a command yet just as compelling, that our enrichment coordinator at Johnson Elementary School, Karen Carroll, has perfected. We are not sure how she does it. She always smiles—you can even hear the smile in her voice over the phone. She never wants to impose. She always knows how much time you've given the school in the past and hates to ask for more. If you can't do it, she's sure she could get someone else, but the teacher did mention you specifically. And she just thought since you're so good in whatever and have such great rapport with the children and if you could be willing to give the time, she would be so eternally grateful and the kids would get so much out of it. It's such a worthwhile activity, and it really won't require that much time or it's so worth whatever time it requires, it would be a shame if the children didn't have this wonderful opportunity.... For some odd reason, nobody can ever say no to the woman. Part of her system must be to never take a breath until she hears the word *yes*.

Another important lesson—one that you will have to relearn and relearn—is to delegate. Get out there and recruit as many people as you can find to help you out. Network with friends, family, neighbors, PTA members, parents of your children's friends. Recruit every warm body you can find. In the beginning, the goal is to get as many people interested and involved in the planning as you can. At the same time, of course, you must be aware of not killing your program before it gets started by releasing a mass of interfering know-it-alls on the school. Choose your committee chairpeople carefully. Look for diplomatic, patient people with empathy and respect for teachers and administrators. One of the best sources of such understanding folk are the former teachers in your neighborhood, temporarily or permanently at home raising their own broods, or retired but not dead above the neck. They're out there and they make perfect volunteers. Few teachers resist the idea of a fellow teacher helping out.

As your program grows, there will arise an increasing need for organization. While we recognize that keeping and filing forms is boring and burdensome, still they are an absolute necessity when organizing large groups of ideas and people. At the beginning of the school year, at the first PTA meeting, at the first parent-teacher conferences, at kindergarten round-up, you need to distribute interest forms to parents to determine what parents are interested and available to volunteer, when, how often, in what sort of capacity. (See the appendix for a couple of excellent examples of interest forms already made up for you by veteran volunteer coordinators around the country.) Respecting your volunteers' requests is important. Let volunteers use their skills as they see fit, at times when they see they can. That doesn't mean you can't ask for more or different later; it means you start off your relationship with mutual respect and trust.

Also as your program expands, so will the need for volunteer training and orientation. Volunteers need to be clear on what is expected of them; teachers need to feel comfortable that the volunteers entering their classrooms will know the rules for acceptable behavior. One cannot depend solely on the volunteer booklet which explains such issues. Just because you give each volunteer a copy of the handbook does not ensure that everyone will read it nor that everyone will understand or see the point in every word. You need to tell each volunteer in person; you need to orient the volunteer to the job, to the building, to the staff, and you need to welcome them formally to the family and make them feel at home.

You do this by planning an orientation meeting at the beginning of the year. Serve refreshments; create a friendly, social ambience. Be friendly, be grateful, but also be authoritative. Communicate professionalism by your behavior. Lead them carefully through every point in the booklet and encourage questions. Take them on a tour of the building. Point out the nurse's office, the teachers' lounge, the coat closet, and so on. Introduce the principal, secretaries, counselor, assistant principals, and others. If specific tutoring or other skills are necessary, set aside time for specialized training.

As well as interest forms, volunteer coordinators need to build card files of all available workers in the community. Keep a file card on every one of your volunteers including their address and telephone number, volunteer commitment, and special skills and interests. Make similar files on every resource person around the community who might be willing to share with children a special interest, a skill, or ethnic-background information. Keep a file of community service and professional organizations, businesses, and industries that have demonstrated a commitment to educational service and that might offer cooperation in the future. For example, in Cedar Rapids, the National Oats Company has frequently donated bags of freshly popped popcorn to schools for popcorn parties or sales; across the country the Junior League has been responsible for initiating hundreds of creative school enrichment programs; and most local police and fire departments have a community liaison person who works with schools in setting up fire prevention, drug awareness programs, and the like. Volunteer coordinators need to keep such information on file for easy access.

Note on each card or entry in what areas it would be appropriate to call on each organization or business. Cross-filing such information may take time and effort, but will prove an invaluable time-saver in the future. Keep a list of volunteers, a list of organizations, and a list of subject areas—a bit like the author, subject, title files in the library—and cross-file all your resources. To help start or add to your lists, consult the appendix for national organizations of interest to volunteer coordinators.

As the program expands, you will need to establish a routine for volunteers to follow when working in the building. We suggest that every volunteer in the building be asked to wear a name tag. Doing so clarifies their purpose in the building to all staff members and is necessary for security reasons. Place the badges on display in or around the main office and ask volunteers to make it a routine to check in with office staff as they pick up their badges. Identify areas in which volunteers may leave their coats and handbags, where it is appropriate for them to work outside the classroom, where they can stop and have a cup of coffee and chat with other volunteers and staff members.

The coffee break issue brings up an important point. Volunteers should feel welcome in the building. Assuming that most programs are not going to have a full-time volunteer coordinator in the building at all times to greet and encourage volunteers, such duties have to be left to other members of the school staff. To facilitate a friendly atmosphere, discuss these responsibilities with your principal. He or she must take a good deal of that responsibility both personally and by directing members of the secretarial and professional staff to always make volunteers feel at home.

Considerations such as where volunteers are to leave their things or take a break must be determined before the issues arise. Many teachers are reluctant to share the teachers' lounge with volunteers. Principals must deal with that issue decisively. It is our view that volunteers must be as welcome in the teachers' lounge as they are in any other part of the building, but we recognize that diplomacy, especially during a volunteer program's infancy, makes special demands. Recommend to your principal that volunteers should be welcome in the lounge, but let the final decision and responsibility rest with the administrator. Should he or she decide against volunteers sharing the teachers' lounge, plan to raise the issue again as soon as it seems appropriate.

Volunteer coordinators must encourage their volunteers to keep good records of the time they donate to the building. In our building—and it seems a very good way to us—there is a sign-up sheet on the same bulletin board as the name tags. Volunteers are asked to sign in each month and then record their hours on a chart each week. At the end of each month, the volunteer coordinator records each volunteer's hour in a record book and logs in the total number of volunteer hours for the month. A new sign-up sheet is hung up and the process begins again.

The statistics thus gleaned are invaluable in evaluating a volunteer program. There should be no need to approximate the number of hours donated by volunteers. You should have it in black and white—or at least a fair if low estimate; invariably some folks will forget to record their hours. To avoid such mental lapses, try to make recording hours simple and routine. By the end of the year or semester, we think you will be amazed at how many hours have been accumulated. Translating hours of service into dollars and cents by multiplying them by wage standards allows you to see what a powerful resource volunteers can be.

Lastly, the volunteer coordinator's most important task is to show appreciation. This anecdote may illustrate the importance of thank-yous. Last Valentine's Day, Melinda received a grocery bag full of hand-made valentines made especially for her by the students she helped with writing. Many little hands painstakingly labored to color and paste lace doilies and stickers on crude hearts cut from construction paper. Inside were notes and verses inscribed in awkward cursive and even more awkward syntax. Her favorite was from Michael, a third-grade baseball player who affected a total lack of interest in poetry but who borrowed Melinda's rhyming dictionary on a weekly basis: "Roses are red, Vilets [sic] are blue, Thanks for helping, Toodle-Loo!"

Melinda's husband arrived home from work to find her reading her cards. As she read aloud her favorites, he picked through the pile as well, smiling at this one or that one and remarking at how much hard work went into each one.

"You know," he shook his head at last. "I'm really kind of jealous. It must feel good to get so much appreciation for the work you do."

"Yes, but Honey," Melinda looked up in surprise, "I don't get paid!"

"No," he said, tossing a card on the table, "but they do say thanks!"

Obviously, that had not been one great day at work for Melinda's husband, but there's more to our little parable than that. The point is that one must never underestimate the value of saying thank-you to volunteers. Appreciation is their only paycheck after all, and one must never forget to fill their pay envelope on a regular basis.

Volunteer coordinators should say thank-you informally after every meeting, every chance encounter, every telephone conversation. Here is another area in which Karen Carroll shines. We can tell you one of her secrets because we have observed it firsthand. She never sees a volunteer enter or leave the building without greeting or thanking the person.

"Sharon," Karen smiles as one of her volunteers strolls into the workroom. "How are you? Is Beth over her cold? Glad you could make it today. We sure appreciate your coming out in all this rain. Have a good day!"

And at the end of a volunteer's duty one might hear, "How'd it go today? Did you have any trouble with those directions? Good. We need more volunteers like you who can handle situations on your own. Thanks a lot for coming. See you next week."

It happens that Karen is a very outgoing, cheerful person by nature; she really does like everybody and really is interested in everything. Those are two very good qualities in a volunteer coordinator. The other important quality Karen possesses is the understanding that volunteers are not her employees. If they can't make it one day or forget their duties occasionally or turn out to be totally unreliable, it is clearly exasperating to her, but she handles it circumspectly. She makes a polite phone call to clear up any misunderstanding, and then it is dropped. No one is berated or made to feel inadequate or as if they have personally offended her. On the other side, everyone who shows up and does a good job is appreciated—every time they do so!

In fact, a good volunteer coordinator will not just say thank-you once, but will mention in one conversation how much your help is appreciated, how well you are handling your job, how the program just couldn't get along without your support—and will even say these things while trying to tell a volunteer that there is a problem. A good volunteer coordinator—or chairperson of a committee or coordinator of an individual program or activity—never fails to compliment her coworkers and is never, never afraid of sounding like an overenthusiastic cheerleader or gushing foot kisser. So your remarks are recognized as so much back patting; admit it. Even the most sophisticated, experienced, cynical volunteer appreciates being appreciated!

Successful volunteer coordinators express their appreciation in more than just words; they also reward their good volunteers with growth. As with any job experience, workers like to feel their expertise is recognized and rewarded. You can't raise a volunteer's pay, but you can reward work well done with promotion. Let experienced volunteers take on more responsibility, deal less with routine, clerical work, become group leaders of other volunteers, and so on.

Thank-you notes should be sent to anyone who has offered some special or outstanding single service: for example, special resource people, guest speakers, and career day participants. Personal notes of appreciation may be written by the volunteer coordinator and/or by the students who benefited from the special program. Nothing warms a volunteer's heart more than sweet, sincere thank-yous scrawled by serious little hands.

An unexpected little note of thanks may just perk a veteran volunteer out of midyear doldrums or avert the onset of volunteer burnout. Never, ever take for granted your loyal, steady volunteer; it may be easy to forget to say thanks to the volunteer who doesn't really seem to need it, who does more than his or her share week after week with nary a mistake or foul-up, who always says yes when you ask, who even asks for more. Look out, that may be the volunteer who needs a pat on the back the most.

We repeat the advice we gave in the last chapter to those trying to break the volunteer ice in buildings where voluntarism is not practiced creatively; never be above a little bribery! There's nothing in the least wrong with "buying" the loyalty of your volunteers; they come pretty cheap actually. An occasional piece of candy or cookie will usually do the trick.

So, at Halloween, put out a bowl of candy for the volunteers with a sign reading: "No tricks about it, our volunteers always deserve a treat!" A pumpkin cookie or miniloaf of pumpkin bread says thank-you at Thanksgiving. Before our winter break, our volunteer coordinator and staff have made it a practice to give Christmas/Hanukkah gifts to each of their some 200 volunteers. No small task, you'll agree. Over the years, they have given a pad of notes with the school emblem printed on each sheet, a tiny jar of homemade jam, hand-crocheted pincushions, a four-inch round of the best peanut brittle you ever lost a cavity to. Each of these offerings was tied with a festive ribbon and accompanied by a clever verse, recipe, or homily appropriate to the gift. Such thoughtfulness really helps keep warm the hearts of volunteers over the winter holiday and ensures their happy, enthusiastic return.

Welcome them back with a New Year's mint and a happy note on the bulletin board: "Be it resolved this new year: Our volunteers are great!" On Valentine's Day, give each volunteer a heart-shaped cookie. Any green goodie—shamrock candies, plant cuttings, cookies—works on St. Patrick's Day. And to ensure that volunteer enthusiasm doesn't start to flag after spring break, hold out the carrot of the volunteer appreciation tea.

Remember that not all of these treats must come from the volunteer coordinator alone. Enlist the support and assistance of the entire staff. In the fall, staff members might sign up for months in which each of them could be responsible for some show of appreciation. Don't leave the students out of the appreciation loop. After all, it is for them that the volunteers are working. Students can and will most sincerely and most willingly offer their thanks, and learning to say thank-you in a variety of ways is an important lesson for all children.

Wait, did somebody mention a volunteer appreciation tea? A tea or some other sort of year-end celebration is a must. It not only makes volunteers feel appreciated, it offers them the valuable opportunity to gather with the staff in a social situation and to talk, laugh, and congratulate each other on a great year. Volunteers will be heartened to gather and appreciate each other and their number. It is the best way to ensure a healthy volunteer program next year. Just remember that the volunteer tea—or luncheon or brunch or coffee or picnic—is given in the volunteers' honor. Guests of honor should not be expected to write out invitations, plan refreshments, shop, or cook for their own parties!

"It makes me just shudder when I think of it!" Sue Pearson, district volunteer coordinator for the Cedar Rapids schools and a normally rather soft-spoken person practically shouts across her desk. "You'd be amazed at the number of schools that do it. Asking the PTA to be in charge of the Volunteer Appreciation Tea! Ridiculous. PTA members *are* volunteers; they shouldn't have to thank themselves!"

Principals, teachers, other administrators and staff members, and paid volunteer coordinators should take the responsibility for organizing such an occasion. *Volunteer* volunteer coordinators may find themselves in the somewhat awkward position of suggesting such an event to school administrators. If you fall into this category, don't be shy; it's important to your volunteer program. Presented that way, we assume any principal supportive enough to have a volunteer coordinator will get the hint.

If the principal or your staff liaison suggests that you go ahead and plan it, well—you can gently point out the irony of that idea if you think you can—or you might just have to go ahead and plan it. However, make frequent, obvious requests for help to the staff. Suggest that monies for gifts come out the school budget, not PTA's. Send out a memo asking teachers to sign up to bring food, decorations, flowers, write a skit or song, draw a poster, make corsages—whatever. While you are working hard to plan this event, make it as transparent as possible that it is the school staff who is thanking the volunteers—including you, certainly—for their year of good works.

To ensure that every parent or community member who offered any kind of help during the year be included in the appreciation tea, we suggest that notes be mailed to outside resource people and a generalized invitation to all parent volunteers be made through a note sent home with every child in the building. This ensures that Bobbie's mom who made cookies eight times and drove on four field trips but never checked in with the office or volunteer coordinator does not get left out of the festivities. Better to make sure Bobbie's mom feels appreciated than worry about Andrea's mother who never lifted a finger all year but shows up at the appreciation tea anyway. If the woman wants a cookie that bad, let her come.

You should try to offer each and every volunteer who comes to the luncheon a special token of thanks—a certificate signed by the principal, a plastic button with thank-you written on it in childish script, a petunia planted in a paper cup by busy kindergarten hands, a thank-you card designed and written by first- through fifth-graders—just a little something that says thank-you to every one. Necessarily such offerings should be inexpensive, easy to produce, nonperishable, possibly reusable (you never know how many will never be claimed), unisex, and preferably involving a variety of staff members and children in their production.

To those who have made outstanding or special contributions to the volunteer program, some special recognition should be made. Those donating a hundred or more hours each year may get a permanent plastic name tag with which hard-working volunteers can "flaunt" their contribution every day it is worn over the next few years. Some who have given a hundred hours of service for more than one year may be "mugged"; with ceramic coffee mugs emblazoned with the school letter. Others giving such extended service may be feted with potted plants, a year's supply of incentive stickers, scented candles, chocolates, distinctive stationery, dried fruit, special soaps, tea towels, or a basket of goodies or any or all of the above.

In Tulsa, Oklahoma, a districtwide salute is held to honor all building volunteers. The program from the 1988 meeting lists all building volunteers of the year and recognizes all volunteers who have donated extensive hours. Their listing *begins* with those who have donated over 100 hours and includes names of those who have donated over 1,000 hours! We're impressed. There are 10 beautiful names on the 1,000 + list.

It is traditional in many buildings to choose one outstanding volunteer of the year. Honor this volunteer with a special certificate signed by the district superintendent and/or an award—perhaps an engraved plaque or trophy to hang in the hall. A formal announcement of the recipient and the reasons for that choice and presentation of the award should be made at the appreciation party. The choice should be publicized in the school newsletter and in any other appropriate publications.

Singling out one person for outstanding service is a tricky business, however. No one wants to stir up bitter feelings in second runners-up who feel they should have been recognized. That's why we suggest making clear the basis on which the decision is based and how the recipient has met the criteria. We also recommend that one of those criteria should be that a recipient cannot win two years in a row. The point of this provision is to avoid the following problem that occurs in many volunteer programs. One outstanding, dedicated soul literally gives her all to her volunteer commitment. He or she must be recognized, but that person may also be an impossible act to follow. We suggest that you do not discourage your other outstanding but less compulsive or less available volunteers by expecting them to meet these unattainable standards.

At the presentation of the award for volunteer of the year, emphasize that the chosen volunteer is really a representative of the entire program and that the volunteer of the year award is an honor in which every volunteer shares and should take pride. Give every volunteer ownership in the award so that it becomes an honor for which to strive, not a source of jealousy, rivalry, or discouragement.

No matter how small or how fledgling the program, all buildings benefit from the privilege of having one central person who coordinates and organizes the efforts of all volunteers and staff members; one person who is responsible for keeping track—of volunteers, of volunteers' hours, of resources people and agencies, of teacher and administrator needs and concerns, and of community needs and resources. Volunteer coordinators should think of themselves as the director of a clearinghouse of ideas, resources, questions, complaints, and suggestions. As Harry Truman declared with a sign on his desk, "The Buck Stops Here." So it is with the volunteer coordinator. The volunteer coordinator in the elementary school is the one with all the answers, the overseer of all the programs, the liaison between staff and parent, a great communicator, and a careful listener.

RESOURCES

Pearson, Sue (volunteer coordinator, Cedar Rapids Community Schools, Cedar Rapids, Iowa). Personal communication, September, 1988.

Salute to Volunteers. Tulsa, Okla.: Tulsa Public Schools, 1987.

School Volunteers: Tulsa Public Schools School Volunteer Program, Development Process. Tulsa, Okla.: Tulsa Public Schools, 1987.

Volunteer Coordinator's Handbook. Cedar Rapids, Iowa: Cedar Rapids Community Schools, 1985.

Wanted: School Volunteers. Tulsa, Okla.: Tulsa Public Schools, 1988.

5 Ah, There's the Rub! Recognizing Resistance

So far, we've been very upbeat about the whole concept of voluntarism in the schools, and for the most part, volunteering in the schools is an upbeat experience. However, we're not Pollyannas, and neither should you be. There is a downside to the picture: resistance. You may encounter it at all levels of the system, from the classroom teacher to the district superintendent. It may come in a variety of strengths and forms. It may be overt or covert. However it is disguised, however deeply it is buried, however direct and insurmountable it seems, resistance must be first expected, second recognized, and third not so much eliminated as gotten around.

Resistant teachers may be intimidated by the idea of having an "outsider" in their classrooms. Do not jump immediately to the conclusion that such a teacher is incompetent and trying to hide something. Yes, it is sometimes true that the less-able teachers are resistant to volunteers because they are unwilling to open their classroom and/or their teaching methods to scrutiny. Such teachers may view the presence of a volunteer as a threat. There are, however, plenty of perfectly capable teachers who work wonderfully and effectively with children, but are still intimidated by the presence of adults. (Maybe, after all, that's why they became elementary school teachers.) There are, as well, very competent teachers who do not wish to give up ownership of their classroom, who view the inclusion of volunteers as an intrusion. Many teachers see volunteers as an addition to their work load rather than as a supportive partner available to carry part of the load: Volunteers need to be trained, need to be led by the nose, demand teacher attention, stick their noses in, don't understand professionalism, and so on.

Be gentle with all such teachers; don't judge them by their objections alone. Try to get a feel for the cause of their resistance and attempt to step into their classroom gently, not over their dead bodies! Follow the strategies we outlined in chapter 3 for approaching your teacher about volunteering in the classroom. Present yourself as a willing, if not silent, partner in the job of educating your child and creating a healthy, happy, creative learning environment. By your example, you can still the teachers' worries about volunteers in the classroom.

As with resistant teachers, resistant principals are neither necessarily incompetent nor complacent. Rather it may be just an indication of inexperience and/or bad past experience. It is, therefore, in your interest to educate them on the pluses of volunteering. You need to reassure such resistant forces that the purpose of a good volunteering program is to act in partnership with the school and to fulfill an enrichment role, not to interfere with or dictate practiced curriculum. We hope this book, particularly this chapter and those dealing with the role of the volunteer and how to establish a volunteer program in buildings where there previously have not been volunteers, will help provide the resources to make convincing arguments for volunteers and/or will direct you to further sources of information about volunteer effectiveness in today's schools.

The forms of resistance you encounter may be direct. A principal, district, or teacher may just outright refuse to allow volunteers to be involved in the school. We would imagine that to be a rare, very unlikely occurrence. Almost every school that we know about involves volunteers in some way. Volunteer usage may be limited in scope; volunteers may only be used to provide transportation for field trips or to sit in a work area segregated from other staff members and cut out letters for the bulletin boards (true!), but there is volunteer involvement of some sort.

Should you come up against a totally belligerent administration, one that sees no use whatsoever for volunteers in the building, we advise you first not to give up. Tread softly and with great respect for principles (principals?) cast in iron, but do not concede the battle. It is possible to overcome such severe resistance. In order to do so, though, you must use every iota of tact and diplomacy in you—and if tact and diplomacy aren't your strong suit, enlist the aid of those in whom they are. Enter the arena armed with information; you must be able to answer the questions of confidentiality and professionalism, you must be aware of concerns about abuse of information, lack of volunteer reliability, responsibility, usable skills, fears of child molesters lurking in the halls. You must be determined and dedicated to your cause; you must believe in it and be willing to work toward your goals with persistence and patience. We think you will be rewarded with a working volunteer program that may just prove to be the pride of your previously resistant staff.

More than likely the resistance you will encounter will be of a more subtle kind. Resistance may show up in the form of regulations that are being strictly—read that restrictively—interpreted. Most school districts define volunteers as being nonprofessional, unpaid school personnel who are subject to the direction of school staff; that is, volunteers do not initiate or define curriculum. That may mean to some that volunteers are not to be involved in any instructional activities and, therefore, not allowed access or involvement with classroom learning activities. We do not believe in such a narrow interpretation. We believe there are many creative enrichment opportunities in which volunteers can contribute to the child's educational experience without interfering with curriculum or the teacher's role as leader in the classroom. It's all in your point of view. So if your principal, teacher, or district resists volunteers on these grounds, try to walk around their narrow thinking and lead them into the fertile grounds of volunteers as enrichment facilitators. That's what reading this book empowers you to do.

You may encounter resistance in the form of meaningless regulations; such as, that volunteers are welcome as long as they do not work in the same classroom as their children. Ho, Ho. Just how many esoteric individuals do you know out there who are just dying to get in there and volunteer simply for the pure joy of volunteering? Not many and certainly not as novice volunteers. Volunteer coordinator Sue Pearson makes the point that one of the things she most enjoyed about being a volunteer coordinator is observing the growth of her volunteers.

They come in at first, shy and unsure, just wanting to help out in their child's room in a very small way. Then slowly their horizons begin to expand to wanting to do more in that room, then more for the school in general, and eventually for the district. I love it when I see someone I know as a parent volunteer at one school who is now on the district list and actively volunteering in many schools.

The broader scope in volunteering must evolve; we cannot expect parents to walk in the door with such philanthropic goals. Initially parents want to volunteer because they are interested in their children, in their children's classrooms, experiences, and teachers. We cannot slam the door in the faces of such willing volunteers because somebody thinks that having parents in the room with their own children would be disruptive. According to the principals and volunteer coordinators we interviewed, there is simply no evidence of that. In case of individual problems—for example, Melinda's experience with her son as we described in the first chapter—we must deal with the individuals. In the broad spectrum, and as in Melinda's experience, children adjust to Mom or Dad being in the classroom and deal with it appropriately.

School personnel may resist the concept of enrichment volunteering simply because it is new to them. It's the old "we've always done it this way" syndrome. There's no place in volunteering for tradition for tradition's sake. There's too much turnover in personnel, in the first place, and too much restriction in that kind of thinking in the second. Each year, in a successful, living volunteer program, there should be many new faces entering the volunteer program bringing with them new ways of looking at things. No ideas for creative volunteering, including the ones outlined in this book, should be carved in stone. We—all of us, volunteers and staff alike—have to be willing to accept change and adapt.

However, one cannot fault school personnel for being human, and it is simply human nature to resist new ideas. We distrust, we fear, we hold at arm's length ideas that are new and foreign to us; so will school personnel. You must overcome their distrust and discomfort with information and familiarity.

Squeeze your way in the door no matter how firmly it appears shut by dealing with what they already know and accept. Make yourself readily and frequently available for traditional needs; pour punch and drive on field trips. As you become a familiar, trusted face, it will become easier and more acceptable for you to suggest a party with a purpose or offer help with classroom tutoring. Then in a few months, it might be feasible for you to present a plan for an Art-in-a-Suitcase program or a Writers Showcase format.

Ingratiate yourself into the system slowly and gently. As you see needs in the building, offer assistance. Cynthia Monroe, principal of Johnson Elementary in Cedar Rapids, Iowa, suggests that one of the safest ways to get your foot in the door of an elementary school is to offer to work in the library media center. Shelving books, checking books in and out are safe, nonthreatening ways to familiarize yourself with the school and vice versa. At least, in these pursuits, you're out of the car or the back room and dealing with students. As the staff gets used to seeing volunteers in that role, they may open up to volunteers in other helping roles around the building and in the classroom.

As you begin to overcome resistance to your presence in the building, you begin to run into resistance on another level, one that may catch you unaware. You as an active volunteer are very likely to be a non-working parent or one who only works part time. In the school you will be working a great deal with staff members who also happen to be working mothers. The debate between these two factions of our society—working mothers versus at-home mothers—is as basic as that between right-to-lifers and pro-choice advocates, atheists and fundamentalists, rabbit hunters and quail hunters. There's no winning any of these arguments, in fact, no point in trying. You just have to accept the inescapable underlying differences in your points of view and respect that.

Still, since there is simply a deep-seated dichotomy of interest between the career-oriented school staff member and the nonworking or part-time employed parent devoted to the concept of volunteering, such feelings may manifest themselves into a subtle lack of respect. "If you were really qualified," considers the staff member, perhaps unconsciously, "you'd be out there getting paid to do real work." "If you were really a good parent," thinks the woman who has chosen to stay home with her kids, "you'd be home taking care of your kids instead of sending them to day care or letting the school be their parents."

Such is the nature of the debate. Neither of the participants may even be aware of their feelings, nor how negatively they affect their relationship. If we confronted those two groups of people and asked them if they harbored any resentment toward each other, they would probably deny it. Take for example this conversation between a volunteer with graduate degrees in education and a professional staff member in the building where the volunteer donates her expertise. "We really need you. You're the best qualified person to do this work," said the staff member referring to the volunteer's contribution, and two sentences later, "So if you have those degrees why aren't you working?"

Yes, this type of resistance is out there. You may very well encounter it. There's not really a darn thing you can do about it, except be aware of it. If you are aware of it, you are more able to let it slide off your back and not deter you from your goals. Just keep these two homilies in mind: "Live and let live," and "Judge not, and you shall not be judged."

Such resistance will also be encountered in closer camps—like the home. No matter how supportive your spouse, your children, your friends, your in-laws say they are, this is still a society founded by the Puritans and firmly planted in the capitalist philosophy. If you are good, you work. If you do good work, you will get paid for it. Your spouse, your friends, your other family members will sooner or later let it slip that they harbor some of those feelings, too. Perhaps it is just a moment of resentment about the fact that you were at school all afternoon and didn't get the laundry done or the beds made or the books back to the library or you couldn't meet for lunch or baby-sit the neighbors' kids—whatever. Had you been busy at a "real" job, others would recognize your business as *work*. But since you were "just volunteering," it doesn't count.

Volunteering is too often looked at as busy-ness or less than that—a time-passer for the idle and/or the rich. We and our fellow volunteers across the country are here to tell you that volunteering is not a pasttime of the rich nor a time-filler for the idle. We are neither rich nor idle; we are volunteers doing valuable and important work acting as partners in our children's education.

You may even find yourself belittling your contribution; falling into the trap our society has set for you. No matter how firmly and completely you believe in what you're doing for its own sake, there will be times when you will doubt your worth. You will refer to yourself in your mind or to others as "just a volunteer." When confronted by a new acquaintance at a party who inquires whether you work, you will say no and accept the look of disapproval in the person's eyes. You will not add proudly that you're an active volunteer. If you do get that confident, you will learn that what follows such an announcement is a patronizing nod of the head and perhaps one quick inquiry while your listener's eyes wander the room searching out intelligent conversation.

Don't let it get you down! Don't let them convince you that volunteering is second-rate. Ask yourself, if I were being paid to do what I do as a volunteer, would I consider it interesting, important, meaningful work? If the answer is yes, then the work you're doing is meaningful, important, and interesting whether you get a paycheck or not! As has been said, "Volunteers may work for free, but they don't work for nothing!"

Fighting off all these obstacles in your way of being a happy, successful volunteer often leads to the biggest resistance of all to volunteering—volunteer burnout. Speaking as two people who have suffered the syndrome at one time or another during our volunteer careers, let us advise you to avoid falling into that pit. It may result in your giving up volunteering. Believe us, that's too drastic a solution for one who has proven—by the fact that you have done enough to burn yourself out—that you are a dedicated volunteer. We can't afford to lose even one of you. So if you or one of your colleagues begins to exhibit volunteer burnout symptoms, take action.

Volunteer burnout symptoms are the same as any other burnout symptoms: job dissatisfaction, feelings of resentment toward colleagues and superiors, absenteeism, failure to do your best, procrastination, frustration, irritability, and feelings of being used or being used up. If you begin to recognize these symptoms in yourself, act quickly. Examine your volunteer commitments. Have you bitten off more than you can chew? Are you working in areas that do not interest you or do not use your unique skills? Are you simply bored with what you're doing? Frustrated by lack of cooperation and support?

Once you have determined exactly how you feel, begin to search for quick, guilt-free solutions. You can't just stop volunteering entirely; that's not fair to your school, the kids, or yourself. Can you cut back? Can you delegate some of your responsibilities or find substitutes to fill in for you? Can you redirect your efforts in areas you would find more interesting and satisfying? Can you discuss your problems with a volunteer coordinator, a staff member, or friend—anyone who will listen sympathetically and be able to offer concrete, specific suggestions? Can you just cry on somebody's shoulder? Misery loves a good listener. Try any and all of these suggestions and begin today. Don't let burnout end your volunteer career. We need you!

If you recognize the symptoms of burnout in fellow volunteers or friends, talk to them. Open the conversation positively and lightly with some remark about how hard they seem to be working. Make the conversation open-ended; let them take the lead at first. Remember to offer lots of praise and appreciation for their efforts; a little pat on the back—or in Traci's case a piece of peanut brittle may be all a tired volunteer needs to heal the burnout wounds. Traci happened to be suffering a little preliminary burnout one day last winter as she trudged into school to fulfill a volunteer duty that didn't particularly thrill her. It was cold out, she was sick, she had a final in algebra the next day, and a scout duty to fulfill that evening. She trudged into the building sniffling, surly, and feeling sorry for herself. Our volunteer coordinator greeted her at school with a bright smile, a sincere thank-you, and large chunk of peanut brittle. The already delicious morsel tasted that much sweeter to Traci. "It was," Traci declares, "the best peanut brittle I ever ate. I really needed somebody to say thank-you that day!"

Severe burnout victims may need more than an encouraging word or a chunk of peanut brittle; they need relief. Offer to help them find ways to lighten their load or redistribute their responsibilities. Maybe they need to redirect their efforts or simply take a vacation.

We hope that these words of wisdom on the problem of resistance will help you recognize it each time it raises its ugly head. Recognizing resistance for what it is and being willing to work with it and around it are half the battle. As you battle resistance, remember that creative volunteering is an asset to any school and you have the *right* to want to make it available to your child and your school. Working cooperatively and respectfully with school administrators should allow you to exercise your parental prerogative.

Part 2
Parties with a Purpose

6 How to Party

A Lesson in Philosophy

When we were kids, the only role parents played at school was that of room mother, and it was always our mother. She baked the cupcakes for the valentine party, drove us to the fire station tour, called other mothers about the PTA meeting. Chief baker and hostess for the classroom party is certainly the most traditional image of the school volunteer, and one that remains active and intact in many schools.

Despite the fact that the next few chapters deal entirely with partying at school, we are in no way sanctioning that old, limiting image. What we are doing is acknowledging that role and seeing it as a springboard to better things. We would like to transform the current concept of a school party into something new and exciting, something with educational value and fun as well. We believe it is not only possible in today's society, but necessary.

We do not believe that children can't have fun and learn at the same time, that children can't have fun and still maintain normal, acceptable behavior, or that children can't have fun without consuming vast amounts of sugar and artificial food coloring. We know it is not necessary because we have experience with both school and private parties at which kids have gobbled nutritious foods, enjoyed interesting, mind-challenging games, and behaved beautifully because they were too busy to do otherwise.

Unfortunately, we have taught our children to expect the wrong things of parties. Ask them what they want to eat at a party and they will list every junk-food concoction known to man. Ask them what they want to do at a party and they will basically tell you run around and make lots of noise and generally behave like children in W. C. Fields's worst nightmare. And that's exactly what you're going to end up with for a party if you take the children's word as gospel. They tell you these things because that's all they know. That's their definition of a *party*. We haven't taught them any better.

Look at our own adult behavior. Take a group of normal, sober, well-meaning, average Americans, tell them it is New Year's Eve and 75 percent of them will feel obliged to drink way too much and act like idiots. The other 25 percent will sit around smiling uncomfortably, fending off clumsy, obligatory passes, laughing at unfunny jokes and staying up way past their bedtimes to blow plastic horns, sing a stupid song, and get kissed on the mouth by people they wouldn't normally shake hands with. No wonder we don't know how to show our kids a good time.

We're not saying we don't want the kids to have fun at their parties. We just want the kids to have fun in a less frenzied way. Let them have fun, for example, eating pizza and milk shakes—two kids' favorites that have some nutritional value. Let them have fun playing games, but make them games that have relevance to a lesson. Let them have fun creating activities and crafts. Let them have fun while learning about other cultures and other times. Let them have fun with their brains as well as their bodies!

Our first premise of partying at school, then, is to teach the kids how to "party with a purpose"; how to have fun and learn something, too. While you're retraining the kids, you may be retraining the teachers and the administrators about how they look at partying. What the parties we will describe in following chapters will do is combine a number of learning activities that are already being used in the schools with the idea of a traditional party, combining work with pleasure so completely that the children can no longer distinguish the two. They'll just think they're having fun.

Always let the kids have fun. That's our second premise. Remember that the party is for the children; not a showcase for your cleverness and creativity. (When a school party is done the way we'd like to see it done, it will require a lot of creativity from the teacher and the parent volunteers, but that is not the purpose of the party.) Let all the kids have fun, not just the most outgoing ones. Everyone in the classroom must be included in planning and participating in the festivities.

One of the best ways to ensure that the kids have fun is let them get involved in the party planning and preparation as much as possible. Although children need leadership and direction, they tend to resent dictatorship. Therefore, the more they are allowed to participate in the party planning, the more comfortable, interested, and enthusiastic they become about the party. They come to the party with clear expectations and no anxiety. Give them as much ownership of the party as possible; let it be "their" party in every sense of the word, and you've pretty much guaranteed everyone a good time. Later in the chapter we will clarify how this can be accomplished in the simplest party and in the most elaborate. In addition, each specific theme chapter will offer suggestions for student involvement.

Be aware that for the most part, surprises are not a good idea. Children like to know what to expect. Surprises tend to make them uncomfortable; they feel threatened; they don't want to participate. We don't mean, of course, that you can't add a little surprise to your party; a special gift or award to the party helpers or the teacher, an added treat, a visit from the principal. Little surprises are fine; just don't take ownership of the party away. Remember it's *their* party, not yours!

We firmly believe that attitude goes much farther than cash. Play on the children's ripe imaginations. If you tell them a four-inch square of green construction paper is a frog, they'll accept that. It's O.K. with them if everything isn't absolutely perfect; as long as you act like you believe that old refrigerator box painted black is a pirate ship, they'll believe it, too. And when in doubt, let the kids do it. Then they'll really believe in what they have created. All this just illustrates the point that elaborate—read that costly—decorations, costumes, and refreshments are *not* necessary to stage a successful, unique party. A willing attitude and a creative point of view will "buy" you a lot more. When you read the specific theme chapters, you will see exactly what we mean.

We see three levels of partying appropriate in the schools. There is the good old, traditional, afternoon classroom party which usually lasts about forty-five minutes and which we are trying to transform from a relatively meaningless school-based sugar high to an interesting learning experience. Next there is the possibility of sponsoring an extended party lasting anywhere from an hour and a half to half a day. The extra time offers the possibility to add a skit or puppet show or other theme-oriented activities and learning possibilities. Lastly, we see the possibility of volunteers coordinating what we call a week-long, month-long, semester-long study unit which culminates in a celebration that uses the students' newly won expertise.

As always, the decision as to which kind of party is most suitable to a classroom is to be determined by the teacher, but we encourage you to offer new possibilities to his or her viewpoint. Depending on the time of year, the age of the class, the topic of the party, and other teacher needs, you could be involved in a classroom party in any of these ways. Don't let the concept of the extended program scare you off; your involvement may not have to be that much more extensive than that required by a creative room party. Relax and read on.

TRADITIONAL PARTY

If you and your teacher decide to go with a traditional party, your commitment will be to plan for that one period lasting forty-five minutes to an hour. You yourself or your recruited helpers will need to organize crafts and activities and provide the food, decorations, and paper products. You should discuss with the teacher exactly what your role is to be during the party—whether you are to be a leader or an assistant.

Every party demands a leader. Either you or the teacher must be in charge. The children expect and want leadership, so don't be afraid to provide it. The leader should explain each activity thoroughly, including the rules, and should have the final voice in issues of controversy. It is the leader who decides when it is time to move on to the next activity, time to eat, time to clean up.

We will discuss specific details of planning your party in the next chapter, but when planning the traditional party, try to pick as creative a theme as circumstances allow or to look at old themes with a new eye. For a "new" twist on Valentine's Day, for example, have an antique valentine collector come to class and share some cards, have the children make valentines for shut-ins or residents of nursing homes, or read them a newspaper article about the origins of the day. It's as simple as that to integrate learning or giving into a party.

Adapt old standby games to your theme. We will show you how to do this specifically in the theme chapters. After you have read about a few of our adaptations, we're sure you'll be coming up with your own. Ordinary games with a new name or a new gimmick aren't stale anymore. Children still love those old standby games—how do you think they got to be old standbys—and kids really get a kick out of playing the clever variations.

On the day of the party, you will have to go in early and set up. Try to do this while children are out of the room if possible or include them in the preparations. Throw a tablecloth over the worktable, trail some crepe paper from the ceiling, hang a couple of balloons, and you're in business. Set out refreshments, so they're ready to be served later.

If you're doing a craft, bring all the materials and have them sorted and ready to pass out. Check with the teacher to see how much precutting or premeasuring needs to be done for this age child.

During the party, if your teacher has given you free reign, direct the activities and crafts with enthusiasm and authority. Do not be afraid of making a fool of yourself. If it is appropriate to moan and swoop around the room, like a ghost, do it! Kids love to see adults acting silly and playing.

We recommend that you wear some sort of appropriate costume. It sets the mood for the kids, adds an extra touch of party flavor, and really allows you to lose your inhibitions. If you already look silly, what's a little moan or swoop here or there?

A word about prizes is appropriate. Winners of activities like to be recognized, but there must be *no* losers. Therefore, everyone must be included in every facet of each game. If it's not their turn to participate, encourage the watching children to cheer for the one competing. Then when a winner is determined, honor the child with a stick of sugarless gum or a sticker, but nothing elaborate. Perhaps at refreshment time, all the winners can be first in line. In addition, try giving rewards for "nonwinning" categories, like best sport, most enthusiastic spectator, and so on. Your attitude counts for a lot in this area. Congratulate each child on his or her achievement as the game proceeds and make every child feel good about his or her participation. If you work it right, if you can encourage enough group spirit, every child in the room should feel as proud of the "winner" as the winner himself.

The end of the party is usually the best time to serve the treats; allow at least ten minutes for eating time. You might want to plan to read a story aloud while the children munch on their treats. Bring treats that are easy to serve and hard to spill. Anything that is already in serving size—a cookie, an apple half, a stuffed celery stick, is better than a snack that must be portioned out during the party. If you want to serve sherbet, for example, scoop each serving into a paper cup, put the cups in muffin tins, and freeze. The day of the party, you just transport muffin tins and use them as serving trays. This is much easier and safer than scooping out sherbet onto droopy paper plates during the party.

Coordinate paper goods with theme of party; these don't have to be fancy. You could just buy plain colored paper goods and decorate them with a suitable sticker or stamp. Just carry the theme through in every way you can.

Stay after the party and help with clean-up. We recommend including the children in this activity as much as possible, but never leave the teacher with a room littered with confetti and juice-filled paper cups. Your whole point is to leave the teacher feeling wonderful and enthusiastic about your volunteer presence, not vowing never to get talked into this again!

EXTENDED PARTY

Your part in hosting an extended party is very similar to that of the traditional party; the primary difference is that there will be more—more time, more activities, more learning, more involvement by the students. Extended parties do not necessarily demand that you have to do more, just that the children will get more!

The great advantage of an extended party is that it allows more time to play with a theme. Children can plan and practice skits and puppet shows to be presented to parents or another class the day of the party. They can get very involved in designing decorations, place mats, bulletin boards, and other simple crafts; resource experts can be brought in to demonstrate crafts or collections appropriate to the theme or to present dramatic programs; and stations can be set up around the room where small groups or individual children can pursue activities or watch demonstrations relative to the theme. The children can become directly involved in such celebrations by planning ahead for these days and coming to school in appropriate costumes. Teachers and volunteers can work together ahead of time to make up fun sheets that correspond to the celebration—crossword puzzles with appropriate terms, coloring graphs of a suitable character, whatever.

Each theme chapter will provide you with more specific directions on how to plan and execute an extended party. Keep in mind that your role will be to act as a facilitator in such a party. You will still be expected to come on the day of the party and to help with preparations and clean-up, but you don't have to feel that you need to do everything—coach the play, design the costumes, bring the activities. Rather your role for this kind of party is to search out local talent and delegate responsibility.

LONG-TERM PROJECT

Long-term projects involve a closer look at a subject that you and the teacher have decided on and in which you both feel the children have an interest. We think such projects would work best if started with a bang—a symbolic ribbon-cutting ceremony on the Book of Dinosaurs, for example—and ended with a climactic celebration of the hard work the children have done.

Any kind of banquet or feast is particularly appropriate to this kind of celebration. Let the children help prepare the food. Try to make the food and the preparation as authentic to the theme as possible. Of course, absolute accuracy is not always possible; that's where you let the children's imaginations take over. For example, a Roman banquet was the highlight of Traci's fifth-grade class. (And we thought we were coming up with new ideas. We guess some of these concepts were in vogue even in the Dark Ages!) She remembers dressing up in Mom's white sheets and dining on such delicacies as hummingbird tongues, quails' eggs, and roast swan. "Actually," Traci laughs, "I think we ate bread cubes, grapes, and olives, but what we were eating was much less important than what the menu said we were eating." Keep those words of wisdom in mind anytime you're planning a children's activity. It's not what it is that counts; it's what you pretend it to be!

Your role in such a project may be to set up a weekly time for a month or a daily time for a week during which you will come to the classroom and work with the students. Or you may just act as a facilitator and find other resource people to contribute time and information. The types of things the children will need help with include research reports, large craft projects—a castle, a log cabin, a dinosaur built to scale, and theme-related books, bulletin boards, and dioramas. Volunteers can assist students with activities that the teacher may not have time to supervise; things like measuring the hallway to see if a dinosaur would fit. Someone will need to work with children to plan a menu, a play, decorations, field trip, costumes, and so on. All of the ideas discussed in the extended party are appropriate here by including the children in the preparations and expanding one-hour projects into week-long studies. Each theme chapter will provide specific suggestions for planning long-term projects.

RESOURCES

Maxted, Traci, and Tomsic, Melinda S. *Happy Birthday Party!* Cedar Rapids, Iowa: 1985 (self-published).

7 How to Party—The Sequel

Planning and Preparation

Now that you have the basic idea of what school partying should be about, let us give some specific advice on how to succeed.

First of all, as in all volunteering experiences, remember that the teacher is in charge. Your role is that of resource person, creative catalyst. The final decisions should always be left up to the classroom teacher, and nothing should be attempted without his or her full understanding and approval.

Therefore, planning the party must be done with the teacher's full approval and understanding. You may have already been asked to host one of the traditional holiday parties in the classroom and wish to spice it up, or you may be suggesting to the teacher a completely new proposal. Either way, remember to approach the teacher with respect and a sharing attitude. You are not telling the teacher how to teach or suggesting curriculum; you are enthusiastic about a new idea and wondering if there's any way it can be fitted into the classroom. Decisions about how elaborate the party will be, whether it will be a two-hour exercise, an all-day enrichment program, or an extended unit culminating in a special celebration are the teacher's decisions.

As you begin the early planning with the teacher, start with a theme. This will be the basis for all the activities, crafts, costumes, foods; it will, in fact, be the purpose of the party. In the following chapters, we will outline a number of themes we find particularly appropriate to the school setting; some in detail, some briefly. We hope that you will view all of our suggestions as jumping-off points and choose a theme for your party that is completely appropriate to the classroom's studies and interests.

If the teacher agrees, this is a great time to get the children involved: Let them pick a theme. You might suggest an area of focus—history, cultural, holiday—and then let them think up the specific theme.

Once you've decided upon a theme, the real party planning begins. A good party, whether at school or home, is based on complete and detailed planning. After deciding how long the party is to be, outline activities that will fill or preferably more than fill, the time allotted. There should never be idle time at a party; never let the children wander about the room or sit unoccupied. At the same time, do *not* feel obliged to make every activity a knockout. Children at a party are much too keyed up to be either overly stimulated or to be left to fend for themselves. Chaos is sure to result in either case, and no one wants to host a mob of bored, over-excited children. If that's not the makings of an Excedrin headache, we don't know what is!

Therefore, you must, like a Boy Scout, be prepared. Plan from the minute you first arrive in the classroom to the minute you leave. Make a chart of the planned activities and approximate time allotted for each. (Later in this chapter approximate times for one round of each activity are provided.) Be sure that you plan a few more activities than you think you'll need.

Vary the activities you plan. Allow for both quiet and somewhat more exuberant activities, passive and active activities, whole-group activities and individual or small-group activities. We recommend that you start the party with a simple, easy-to-follow, but engrossing group activity such as a craft or costume making to put to best use the pent-up enthusiasm the children feel at the beginning of the party; follow that with a couple of moderately active games; then one very physical game, return to a group activity, perhaps a passive one like listening to a story, a skit, or other presentation, then end the party with refreshments. This arrangement results in a logical flow of activities from quiet to moderately active, to rambunctious and back again. A general party agenda should look something like this for an extended party lasting an hour and a half:

12-15 min.:	craft or costume making
10 min.:	hunt
15 min.:	two stand-in-line games
15 min.:	racing games
10-15 min.:	play or presentation
15 min.:	refreshments
10 min.:	clean-up

When you are setting up your agenda, be sure to allow time for "nonactivities." Things like reading directions to nonreaders, explaining crafts and activities, pouring and passing refreshments, sorting groups or equipment, dressing younger children into and out of costumes, and gathering up goodies to take home. All of these nonessential activities take time; plan for it.

On the following page is a sample agenda for a forty-five-minute Halloween party for first- and/or second-graders.

ACTIVITIES

Few of the games we list here will be new to you. These are the games of our childhood, of our parents' childhoods, probably of their parents' childhoods. They are the tried-and-true favorite games of children. We simply update them with a theme-related gimmick; we dress up old dogs in new hats, so to speak, and let their basic charm enchant the children as these simple games and activities have done for generations of children. After all, if kids didn't like htese games, they wouldn't have lasted so long! Using games that are familiar to most of us also has the advantage of simplifying the explanation process, both from us to you and from you to the kids.

Another excellent way of entertaining a whole classroom of children is to divide them into smaller groups and set up stations of activities around the room. You may, for example, set up an activity in each corner of the room: In one corner children are making place mats or hats, in another they are playing a game, in the next they are listening to a story, and in the last, they are playing another game. Every five or ten or fifteen minutes, all the children leave their stations and go to the next. You and the teacher can either supervise a station and recruit two other parents to help, or you may have set up self-help stations and you and teacher can float around the room. As we describe the activities, we will note those that adapt well to the station concept.

A couple of words of wisdom: Plan to play only one round of each game when you are making your agenda, but when the party rolls around, the kids may want to play seventeen rounds of Pin-the-Tail; let them. They may not enjoy the next activity half as much. Be flexible.

We have listed the games according to categories: quiet games and crafts, running or active games; and stand-in-line games. We have also included approximations of the time one round of each game will take, but remember that these are estimates. Class size, abilities, number of helpers, personalities of kids, and any number of other factors can all influence how long an activity will take. We recommend talking over your plans with the teacher and discussing time approximations.

Halloween Party — classroom

NOTE: Children will be at all school costume parade. Set up then go out to take pictures.

NOTES:	ACTIVITIES:	TIME:	EQUIPMENT:
set-up	decorate — hide clues for hunt	15min pre-party	white balloons, markers for faces, clues, prizes for hunt
	class return from parade — help w/costumes. Make-up scars & pumpkins	10min.	orange & red clown make-up treat to show,
any colorblind?	divide into 3 groups explain clues	5min.	color coded clues w/ pix
	Hunt	6 min.	
→	by groups — assembly line style get treats — out of costumes while waiting put faces on cookies eat treats, tell ghost story as eat	10 min. 10 min.	orange-frosted cookies, choc. chips, candy corn, toasted coconut, parents' treats bags for extra treats, napkins, punch, cups
teacher knows method	clean-up	5 min.	garbage bag

stay & do real clean-up if necessary.

Quiet Games and Crafts

Lotto. Ages three to eight, depending on difficulty of the game. This game adapts well to themes and is easy to construct. Using stickers, cutouts from color books, or the artistic talents of the students, make a Bingo board. For small children, make the board three squares by three; for older children, increase the number of squares. Make enough copies for each child in the class or for the number that will be at this station at a time. Then cut up the originals and glue all but one of them in random order on new sheets of paper so that each board is different. Keep one set of symbols to draw from a hat during the game. Older children may help with this step. For markers use traditional ones: little scraps of paper; or miniature marshmallows, red hots, M & M's, raisins, peanuts, or even popcorn, and the children can eat their markers when they're finished playing. (Beware of older children or rambunctious groups who may use such items as flying missiles.)

Then play Lotto, just as you play Bingo. One round of Lotto will take five to ten minutes; add another five or ten if students are making boards. This game adapts well for use at a station, but note that there needs to be a leader, a "master of ceremonies," to draw the symbols from the hopper and announce them to the players.

Bingo. Ages six to twelve. Buy a game—check with your PTA or school principal; it's quite likely your school owns a Bingo game. To adapt Bingo, change the letters B-I-N-G-O to suit your theme: W-A-G-O-N for frontier days or S-A-U-R-S for dinosaurs.

Crafts. (Teachers are great resources for crafts; they may have one perfect for your theme, so be sure to check with them for really creative ideas.) Here are some of our generic suggestions that can be adapted well to any theme.

- Make your own place mats, hats, vests, props, goody bags, or decorate the above.

- Decorate your dessert—cookies, cupcakes, or ice cream dips. Provide plain, already iced cupcakes or cookies or plain ice cream dips, small bowls of raisins, M & M's, colored sugar, cake decorations, marshmallows, chocolate chips, Cheerios, and so on, and let the children create their own decorative designs.

- Art contest—children draw whatever or something appropriate to the theme. It's even more fun to think up silly, fun, or appropriate categories for awards: "Greenest Dinosaur" or "Best Use of the Color Purple."

- Peanut butter playdough—a great little recipe for edible playdough, for children ages four to seven. They will get a real kick out of really eating their handmade pancakes, cakes, and pies!

  1 small jar peanut butter

  4-5 cups powdered milk

  Add powdered milk to peanut butter until it's no longer sticky. If your mixture gets too dry, add a little water, milk, or honey to make it pliable.

Shapes and straws. Ages five to nine. Cut small shapes suitable to the party theme—hearts, strawberries, pirate patches, geometric shapes—out of construction paper. Cut regular plastic straws in half. Provide each child with a small paper plate, a straw, and five, ten, or twenty (depending on age) cutouts. The child must use the straw to suck the shapes off the table and release them onto the plate. The first one who transfers all the shapes is the winner. Time: three to five minutes.

Fun sheets. There are any number of fun (rather than *work*) sheets that can be made up ahead of time and adapted to a theme. Crossword puzzles (some computers have programs for making up crosswords), word searches, color-by-number pictures, graph coloring, coloring sheets are all appropriate activities for a party. Ask your teacher for ideas and/or check in teacher-oriented work booklets for already made-up, ready-to-mimeo work sheets that suit your theme. Fun sheets can also be used as take-home party favors.

Word games. Ages six to eleven. Those old stand-by parlor and car games we learned as children are great entertainers for the older children, such as Twenty Questions; I'm Going on Vacation (Begin with the phrase "I'm going on vacation and I'm taking a suitcase"—or whatever. The next participant repeats, "I'm going on vacation and I'm taking a suitcase and a dog." The next in line says, "I'm going on vacation and I'm taking a suitcase and a dog and a swimsuit," and so on around the room until someone is stumped and can't remember the sequence. You can adapt this game easily to theme by changing destination and insisting all items must be relevant. For example, "I'm going to the Wild West and I'm taking my horse," etc.); Add-a-Line Story (Start a group off with the opening line of a story and let each person add one line. The point is to try to keep the story fun, interesting, and logical as long as possible.); Charades; I Spy (something that starts with the letter....); or any other of the games your parents tried desperately to divert you with on long car trips. Kids find them really fun at a school party. Time: Ten minutes.

Puzzles. Ages four to eight. You can make puzzles from greeting cards that suit the theme or copy appropriate pictures and paste them on card stock and then cut them out in odd shapes. You may allow older children to cut their own puzzles. Time: Five minutes.

Entertainments. These include such activities as reading stories aloud, songs, puppet shows, skits, or any other sort of performance. Remember to look beyond your own skills. For example, does your neighbors' teen-age son dabble in magic? Maybe he could help!

Keep any sort of plays or puppet shows short and simple. Three to six minutes is plenty of performance time. Plays can be taken from classroom reading books, any of the wonderful drama books in your local children's library, or a fairy tale or folktale adapted into a drama expressly for the party. The simplest form of drama is to let one person be the narrator reading from the script and other members of the cast simply pantomime action.

Plays performed by the class are probably best suited to the extended party or the long-term project. As always, clear everything with the teacher, then let the kids do as much as possible. You can act as cheerleader, prompter, perhaps director, but let the kids do the rest.

Keep costumes simple and let the kids do it! Remember that a pile of large fabric pieces and a few belts will take you far! A general purpose pack of theatrical makeup is a great investment for any mom or active volunteer and will take you through many, many performances. It's well worth the ten bucks you may spend on it. Other than that, save your money.

There are scores of great books on puppet construction and puppet shows, so if you are planning a puppet show, check out your school or public library. Scout leaders and their literature are also good sources of information. In general, paper lunch sacks and crayons will provide all the materials you need for quick puppets. You can augment these simple characters with bits of fabric, trimmings, buttons, glue-on eyes, yarn, and so on. And at show time, don't be surprised that some of your stage-shy young actors prove to be darned good puppeteers!

Active Games

Before you plan any of these more rambunctious activities, be sure to check with the teacher on the suitability of such games. The best possible choice for many of the more physical activities would be to play them on the playground or in the gym. The following are slightly rowdy games that we think would be suitable for the classroom.

Hunt. Any age, depending on the difficulty. This game is exactly what it says, a hunt. Younger children need to know exactly what they are to find and where to find it and how many they are to find. Use clearly distinguishable items that are suitable to the theme and scatter them in plain sight. For older children, increase the difficulty: Hide the items more cleverly, use written clues, use picture clues, and try cryptic clues or rhyming clues for the oldest groups. Time: Five to ten minutes (very variable, depending on difficulty, but never lasts nearly as long as it takes you to prepare it or as long as you expect it will!)

Races. There any number of variations on the race. Relay races work best for large groups. Variations on the straight race include running to some point and doing a stunt of some sort, passing an obstacle, pushing an object with a stick or a broom, running with something hard to carry (dried beans on a plastic knife). One of our favorites is the Shoe Race. Have kids remove shoes and put them at the far end of the relay course. Line them up at the start line. At signal, they run to shoes, put them on, lace them, tie them, then run back to start line. You can vary this by having them put on and button a shirt, or a silly hat, or an apron, any combination thereof, or any of the specific items we suggest in the theme chapters. Time: Five minutes.

Follow the Leader. Ages four to seven. We all know how to play this—so do the kids. It's usually best that you always be the leader, so that you control the action and no one feels hurt if there's not time for everyone to have a turn at being leader. Time: Five minutes.

Simon Says. Same as above.

Parade. Ages four to six. Again, the name is self-explanatory, and we all know how to march. The only thing we wish to add is that the parade adapts easily to a number of themes and that it's really fun for children to parade through the halls of the school showing off their party costumes and theme. (Guess what—check with teacher before you plan one!)

Duck, Duck, Goose. Ages four to seven. You may call this game Drop the Handkerchief or something else. It is the game where everybody sits in a circle, facing in. *It* runs around the circle, touching heads, saying, "Duck, duck, duck," until he reaches who he wants to be It next. Then he says "Goose," and races around circle to that person's place. The child he's chosen chases him around trying to tag him before he gets back to place. If the first child makes it back to the place without being tagged, the new child is It. Otherwise the original It has another turn. Of course, this one adapts well to every theme. Time: 5 minutes.

Musical Chairs. The great thing about musical chairs is that it is so easily adapted just by calling chairs animals or other objects and playing music appropriate to the party theme. Time: Five minutes.

Stand-in-Line Games

We call this set of games *stand-in-line*, but our first word on them is *don't* have kids stand in line. Tell them to make a circle and encourage them to cheer for every participant. All of these games adapt well to the station concept; in fact, we recommend breaking a class into small groups to play these games.

Pin-the-_____-on-the-_____. Ages five to ten. Again, we think no explanation is necessary for this old stand-by. Is there anyone out there who never played Pin-the-Tail-on-the-Donkey? This is the same game; we're just very flexible about what you pin and what you pin it on. Maybe you pin a patch on the pirate or ten-gallon hat on a cowboy; whatever suits your theme. Our only change is, don't *pin* anything: Use masking tape. Young children may be frightened of the blindfold; don't force it. They have just as much fun pretending to close their eyes. You can increase the difficulty of this game for older children by making the object to pin and its target smaller. Time: Seven to ten minutes for a group of six.

Clothespins in the Bottle. Ages four to ten. The original version of this game is pretty much what the name says. Participants attempt to drop clothespins into the mouth of a bottle. Try this at home; it's harder than it sounds! You will find that we adapt this basic concept for any number of themes. Time: Five to seven minutes.

Bean Bag Toss. Ages five to ten. This is another self-explanatory game which we have all played and which many a carnival shark has made a few bucks on. Again, one can increase or decrease the difficulty of this game by changing sizes of the targets and the distances from which bags must be tossed. To make this game less competitive for young children, let each child toss bags until he or she gets one in the target. Time: Five to seven minutes for six children.

Dog and Bone. All ages. This may sound new to you, but read on. You probably just never knew it by this name. *It* is the "dog" and stands in front of the class, with It's back to the other children. The "bone" is any object placed behind the child to be snatched by another "dog." In one version, the It dog turns around when he hears someone sneaking up to grab the bone. If the dog catches the thief, they exchange places. Another version has the It dog wait until the class says ready. While the dog's back was turned, the thief has taken the bone, returned to his or her place, and put the bone in his or her lap. The dog then turns around and tries to guess — by the innocent looks on their faces — who is the thief.

Seven-Up. All ages. Seven-up is really just another variation on Dog and Bone. In this case, though, seven people are It and stand at the front of the room. The rest of the class puts their heads down on their desks with hands out in a loose fist. Each of the Its must put up a thumb of one of their classmates and return to the front of the class. Then the classmates guess which It pulled up their thumbs. If they guess right, they get to be an It and the game continues.

RESOURCES

Brownie Girl Scout Handbook. New York: Girl Scouts U.S.A., 1986.

Childcraft: The How and Why Library. Chicago, Ill.: Childcraft International Inc., World Book, 1981.

Cub Scout Leader How-To Book. Irving, Tex.: Boy Scouts of America, 1988.

Maxted, Traci, and Tomsic, Melinda S. *Happy Birthday Party!* Cedar Rapids, Iowa: 1985 (self-published).

McCall's Golden Do-It Book. New York: Golden Press, 1960.

McNeice, William C., and Benson, Kenneth R. *Crafts for Retarded.* Bloomington, Ill.: McKnight and McKnight Publishing, 1964.

Peter, John. *McCall's Giant Golden Make-it Book. New York: Simon and Schuster, 1953.*

Pointillart, Marie-Blanche. Costumes from Crepe Paper, Little Craft Book Series. New York: Sterling Publishing, 1974.

8 About Last Week and the Dinosaurs

Historical Parties

History, in the eyes of the elementary student, includes everything from the events of last week to the era of the dinosaurs. Time has little meaning to children; the 1930s seem as distantly past to them as the Middle Ages or the days of the Roman Empire. While classroom teachers frantically try to find enough time in the day to teach reading, writing, 'rithmetic, music, art, P.E., skills for growing, plus a dabbling of science and geography, history is often a subject for which there just isn't enough time. It is an area ready-made for the volunteer; an important academic field of study just ripe for some volunteer enrichment.

Not ones to let such a good thing go by, we see the historical perspective as a wonderful opportunity for the creative volunteer to introduce enrichment into the classroom through the completely nonthreatening avenue of hosting a party. In this chapter we provide detailed outlines for hosting traditional classroom parties, sponsoring an extended day event, or supporting a long-term project using three historical periods as your base; Dinosaur Days, Medieval Festival, and Frontier Fair. We will also suggest other themes and/or time periods that would adapt well to these purposes with a little of your own creative input.

DINOSAUR DAYS

Every specialty and/or toy shop in the mall carries a line of dinosaur somethings. Dinosaur stuffed animals, dinosaur blow-ups, dinosaur coloring books, dinosaur books for every reading level, dinosaur board games, dinosaur action figures, dinosaur plastic and paper tableware, dinosaur pens and pencils, dinosaur stickers, dinosaur posters, dinosaur hats, dinosaur T-shirts, even dinosaur-shaped cookies and cookie cutters. Natural science and history museums across the country are featuring their dinosaur exhibits currently. During 1988-1989, for example, a traveling exhibit of mechanical dinosaurs toured museums across the Midwest accompanied by much hoopla and dinosaur-oriented merchandise. Dinosaurs are definitely *in*.

Why the sudden interest in a creature extinct for fifty million years? Kids have been fascinated by dinosaurs for generations, but now for some reason Madison Avenue has caught on and turned that natural curiosity into a fad. Who knows why. Naturally, the authors figure it's because our children have grown out of their passionate interest in the creatures; six years ago when our boys were fixated on dinosaurs, none of the current goodies were available. Our advice to teachers and volunteers with a future: Stock up now. This is definitely a trend and trends don't last. We predict that two or three years from now dinosaurs may become as extinct in the malls as they did on the planet a few millennia ago.

There are any number of easy, fun ways to specialize parties using the dinosaur theme. Thanks in part to Madison Avenue and the current national interest in the beasts, more children of all ages will be interested in a party with a dinosaur theme. The following are ways in which you can build a party around the very historical beast, the dinosaur.

Traditional Party

Because of the time constraints, the best way to incorporate a specific theme into a short class party is through the treats or snacks served. As we mentioned, dinosaur-shaped cookie cutters are readily available at kitchen and/or hardware stores—wherever cookie cutters are sold. Using any rolled cookie recipe, you can mass-produce a clan of edible Tyrannosaurus Rexes, stegosauri, and/or triceratopses. You can decorate these with icing—or leave this step as a party activity for the kids. Even lazier room mothers, like Melinda, can buy dinosaur-shaped animal crackers and graham crackers. Outline the grahams in white frosting, and Melinda thinks you've done your duty—besides, they taste a lot better than any cookies she'd bake!

For a more thoughtful twist on the refreshments—perhaps more appropriate for upper grade levels who get the significance—serve treats the creatures might have enjoyed themselves. A green salad or veggies tray for all the vegetarian dinosaurs; some sliced hard-boiled eggs for the carnivores served on "bark" (crackers or whole wheat bread).

Remember, during a traditional party, you will only have time for one or two activities.

ACTIVITIES

Active

Follow the Dinosaur. Children walk like dinosaurs, eat leaves, roar, swish their imaginary tails, lumber around, and generally make brontosauri of themselves. Most appropriate for younger ages.

Hunt. A hunt of dinosaur shapes is appropriate for all age levels, depending on how cleverly the shapes are hidden. For older kids, different dinosaurs could be represented by shape, and they could be required to gather one of each type and be able to identify their finds. "Fossils" in the forms of plastic or paper cut-out bones could be the object of a hunt.

Pterodactyl, Pterodactyl, Rex. This is just Duck, Duck, Goose with more syllables.

Stand-in-line

Toss. A dinosaur toy of some type—a small stuffed animal, a miniature blow-up, or an action figure—can be dropped or tossed into a bucket, which you may call the dreary swamp.

Relay race. For the Dino Romp, have children wear paper grocery sacks on their feet, then shuffle their way to the finish line.

Pin-the-Tail-on-the-Dino or **Pin-the-Tooth-on-the-Tyrannosaurus-Rex.** The latter gives little ones a little more leeway as there is a larger target area in which teeth might be placed. You may be able to augment your artistic skill by using a dinosaur poster of some sort as the background and just cut out a tail from green construction paper.

Dino and the Bone. Play this as you do Dog and Bone.

Quiet

Fun sheets. A coloring sheet of a dinosaur for younger kids, a work sheet about dinosaurs for older kids.

Read a story about dinosaurs.

Make a dinosaur bookmark. Have bookmarks already cut out from construction paper and let kids make their own saurial designs.

Shapes and straws. Cut out dinosaur footprints or dinosaur silhouettes for the shapes.

Lotto. Use different dinosaurs, dino eggs, bones, footprints, trees for the shapes on the board.

Decorations can consist of putting up dinosaur posters around the room. Such posters are available through museums and teacher-supply stores or catalogues. We suggest simple dinosaur posters for younger children, more educational posters such as charts of types of dinosaurs and/or geological age charts for older children.

If you'd like to add something extra to the treat table, make a palm tree out of crepe paper fronds hanging from a cardboard tube trunk. As we mentioned, it is probably quite possible to buy appropriate paper products, but you could also use one or more of the wide variety of dinosaur stamps or stickers to decorate napkins, cups, and/or plates.

To add that special touch to your party, you could use clown makeup to paint a dinosaur footprint on little hands or cheeks; you could don a dinosaur hat or T-shirt or just dress all in green and tie some spikes along your back or wear a tail. Learn some dinosaur riddles and jokes to break the ice or add spice to the boring punch-pouring moments.

Extended Party

All of the above advice holds true for an extended party, but instead of picking just one activity, one refreshment, and one decoration, you can choose a couple or three of each. Bring several posters for decoration, have veggies and cookies, and play one of each type of activity.

In addition, extended parties allow time for more elaborate creative and craft activities. You are, for example, able to have children in any grade act out a story about dinosaurs that you read aloud. Or you could measure dinosaurs. You or the children could research the length of various kinds of dinosaurs; a poster might provide such information. Then in groups, take children to the hall to measure how much room the dinosaur would take up. You could mark the lengths with crepe paper streamers on ceiling, masking tape on the floor, chalk marks on the wall. You might also want to display various other sizes—sizes of different kinds of eggs, footprints, heads, feet, tails, and so on.

Children from first through sixth grades might enjoy making their own fossils out of plaster of paris. To create their fossils, put about an inch of mud or clay in the bottom of a small paper cup. Press item to be fossilized into the mud—a leaf, rock, bone—then take it out again. Make sure that it has left an imprint in the clay. Next pour one-half to one inch of plaster of paris on the mud and let it dry. When dry, tear off paper cup and remove mud or clay to uncover your plaster fossil.

Little ones in kindergarten through second grade may make dinosaur tracks. Fill an old pie pan or dishpan with a half-inch or so of tempera paint. Let the child dip his or her bare hand or foot into the paint and then on to construction paper or long roll of brown paper. Be sure to have bucket of warm water and towels handy. An extra pair of hands wouldn't hurt on this one, either.

Long-Term Project

As with most long-term projects, we recommend that the Dinosaur Days long-term project be limited to children in upper grade levels; therefore, we aim all our suggestions at children in third through sixth grades.

Make a dinosaur. We know it is possible for elementary children to make a half-size papier-mâché dinosaur because some hardworking little hands in our school did just that—with the help of their patient and creative teachers and parents. We are not about to give full directions for building one of these. Besides the fact that we don't know how, we think that would take half the fun out of it. If you and your teacher and kids are of a mind to undertake such a project, we think you must be of the spirit who likes to do it yourselves; far be it for us to interfere. Good luck!

For those of you with less elaborate aspirations, there are a number of other ways to make a dinosaur. Each child, for example, might model an individual project out of clay or playdough. Or groups of two or three children could work together building models accurate to scale and other physical details. Besides being molded from clay, models could be constructed from papier-mâché, carved from bars of soap, folded from paper origami-style, built with Legos, drawn on blueprint or regular paper, or painted on poster board or canvas.

Students could be assigned research projects and/or creative stories to be presented to the class or displayed on the last day. Again children could work in groups, each working on a separate type of dinosaur or a different way to present facts about dinosaurs. Some students might want to write a play or the script for a docudrama about the creatures. Some might want to build a diorama that displays the ecosystem of their dinosaur.

Using the station idea outlined in chapter 7, students might want to work in groups and set up different stations for each day of the week or each week of the month. One station could have a trivia game involving knowledge of dinosaurs. The next one could be a crossword puzzle. The next week a group could have made available all the books in the library or a selection of books about dinosaurs. Let your, the teacher's, and especially the children's imaginations be your guide. Brainstorm as a class about what sorts of things could be done. You'll be amazed at the enthusiasm and problem-solving skills as well as group cooperation that can be illustrated by such a project.

Younger children might enjoy making and coloring dinosaur cutouts for the calendar. Children of all ages could design dinosaur bulletin boards that illustrate the environment of the dinosaur, including vegetation, water sources, and weather. Another bulletin board idea would be to graphically display the geological ages and the creatures who lived in each. A fun project that may stimulate your class clowns would be to take a leaf from Gary Larson's cartoon of cigarette-smoking dinosaurs and let the kids think up their own silly reasons for the demise of the dinosaurs and illustrate them in cartoons.

MEDIEVAL FESTIVAL

With this party theme, children step back into the period of time in which some of our most famous heroes, real and legendary, lived. The Medieval Festival is an event that would have been a celebration in the lives of King Arthur and the knights of the Round Table, Robin Hood and his Merry Men, King Richard the Lion-Hearted, the crusaders. It is the world of castles and princesses in distress, Cinderella and Sleeping Beauty, the Princess Bride, knights in shining armor, and the fire-breathing dragon. What better material for an imaginative, fun, children's party could one wish for? And they might even learn something, too—but you don't have to mention that until later!

Traditional Party

This might be a good school party in the early spring when some activities could be held outdoors. you could also tie in the idea that while we in modern times are observing our spring holidays—Easter, Passover, Mardi Gras—people in the Middle Ages—or Dark Ages as they were called—celebrated their own sort of spring rites, usually at the medieval version of a carnival.

At such a fair, food delicacies would be sold from carts or booths; such dishes as fresh fruits, meat pies, and pastries. So for snacks at your party, you might serve orange sections, apple or pear slices, a hard roll scooped out and filled with beef stew, individual cherry tarts, or pies of any sort, homemade bread, hot cross buns, scones, and so on. Remember to keep sweets at a minimum as sugar was rare in these times. Apple cider would be an appropriate drink.

In these Dark Ages, even refined folk used dogs for napkins—they called the dog and wiped their hands on its fur. (Yuck). Tell the story as you pass out napkins; the children may refer to their napkins as dogs. To keep up the authenticity, especially with older children, pass out forks but no spoons.

For younger children, keep it very simple and just serve cookies in the shapes of shields or dinosaurs and call them dragons.

ACTIVITIES

Active

Balloon sword fights. Group children for control. Give one long, narrow balloon to each sword fighter and let them duel briefly—perhaps until the sand runs out on a one-minute timer.

Knight, Knight, Knave. This is a variation on Duck, Duck, Goose.

Shoe race variation. Use old shirts of fathers or the class paint shirts and call them armor—or make an "armor" breastplate and back protector from cardboard sprayed with silver paint. In a relay have children don their armor, then take it off for the next child to use.

Hunt. Go on a hunt for game. Find cutouts of deer, poultry, boar, and others.

Stand-in-line

Bean Bag Toss. Toss bags into a "turret" made of paper-covered coffee can.

Pin-the-Sword-or-the-Shield-on-the-Knight. Or Pin-the-Fire-into-the-Dragon's-Mouth. Or Pin-the-Sword-on-the-Dragon's-Heart. Check out your specialty gift and record shops for appropriate posters.

Quiet

Make costumes. The younger children will enjoy creating their own medieval headgear. Girls can make ladies' hats by making a paper cone out of pastel or brightly colored construction paper and attaching a tissue-paper train to the tip. Boys can make armored helmets by cutting a face hole out of a paper bag. To make it look more realistic, try cutting narrow vertical rectangles at eye level and horizontal strips for nose and mouth.

Shapes and straws. Cut out shields, ladies' hats, dragons, castles, turrets, pennants, or combinations of the above.

Lotto. Use the themes listed above as well as glove, sword, and helmet for lotto symbols.

Read a story about princesses or knights or King Arthur.

To add the festive spirit to the room, festoon it with brightly colored banners and pennants. Older kids could decorate these with family crests of their own design. Tableware could be in bright colors with stamps or stickers of shields or dragons, or any products featuring princesses or knights. You might want to wear a long skirt, anything velvet, a brocade vest, or a fancy hat to suit the theme.

Extended Party

Involving the children in the food preparation is particularly appropriate for an extended party of this theme. Let them make their own "trenchers" by hollowing out the rolls for the stew. Let them help prepare the stew using hamburger or precooked beef and canned veggies. Remember to use as many wooden and/or crockery cooking utensils as you can.

Older children may build their own castles in small groups. Provide variously sized small boxes and cans; sugar cubes; toilet paper, paper towels, and wrapping paper tubes; clay and/or playdough; construction paper; glue—and see what these architects can produce in thirty minutes.

Students may act as players in a story you read aloud. Any folktale or even Bible story would be appropriate, since that is the drama the people watched at their festivals.

Designing banners, mobiles, or bookmarks would be a good craft project for any age. Dragon bookmarks are particularly appropriate to this theme. Older children might enjoy designing their own crests.

Long-Term Project

One of the best ways to turn this into a long-term project is to present the party as the market day or festival day, and the weeks or month before as preparation for that day. Students may divide into groups or work independently on projects to get ready for the festival. Older students may do library research on, for example, foods, costumes, lifestyles, weapons, and class structures of this time period. Younger children may be read stories, shown movies or filmstrips, or read to from the encyclopedia about this time period. Pertinent projects for this type of party would be to design banners, costumes, coats of arms or build castles, catapults, or suits of armor. Children may want to write their own folktales, plays, or ballads. Younger children may draw pictures of people, houses, towns, and fairs as they would have looked during this time. Other projects could include making or completing work sheets about the period—word finds, crossword puzzles, coloring graphs that reveal an item used in that time period—doing book reports and movie reviews on books and films pertinent to this study, or making a dictionary of Middle Age language and terms unfamiliar to people today.

In preparation for the day, resource material may be gathered and made available to students. Books and poems about the legends of King Arthur and Robin Hood should be made available or read aloud to children. Movies such as *Camelot, The Sword in the Stone,* or any of the many *Robin Hood* films or television shows, and *The Princess Bride* are available at video stores and could be used either as study resources or as a special treat on festival day. Have the children take note of the differences between various versions of the same legends or the differences in what they learned about what life was actually like and the way they see it depicted in the movies.

Perhaps the class could divide into groups, with one group responsible for researching and preparing several craft items or baked goods to be sold at their booth during the class Scarborough Fair. You can provide resource materials and/or lists of items that might be appropriate—any of the foods listed under refreshments would work. Craft items could include ladies' pointed hats and/or attached scarves, banners, shields, coats of arms, bows and arrows, and leather or felt pouches.

Each child might design a personal coat of arms on a cardboard shield: After dividing the shield into fourths or thirds, the child could draw pictures or cut them from magazines to reflect in the sections his or her interests and background. Younger children might enjoy coloring dragons already drawn on work sheets; middle grades might like creating their own monsters from scratch.

Interesting topics for individual research or class discussion would include armor—who wore it, when, and why; castle design and construction—why, for instance, did they all have spiral staircases?; governmental philosophies—the feudal system, "might makes right"; and/or the code of honor of knights.

Decorations around the room should reflect the period. Banners and pennants could be suspended from the ceiling. Remnants of brocade fabric could be hung on the walls like tapestries. Bulletin boards could be used for displaying "proclamations" written in Old English lettering that announce coming events in class.

There are any number of ideas for stations appropriate to this theme. Such stations could be set up by students, teachers, volunteers, or a combination working together. One station might allow the students to practice their calligraphy skills and mimic the writing styles of the period. Included at such a station would be a book illustrating the Old English alphabet, a book illustrating pages from hand-copied books of the Middle Ages, ink and pens or quills, heavy paper on which to practice, and a blotter. Another station might just have a variety of books on castles in Europe. Folktales might be a theme of another station, available for children to read or listen to on tape. From these they may draw inspiration to write their own tales which could also be left or displayed at the station. Another station might deal in the music of the times. Instruments such as flutes, recorders, mandolins, and guitars could be set out for strumming or tooting. Tapes of minstrel songs, madrigal singers, and folk singers could be available for listening. Vocabulary lists explaining musical terms such as ballad and minstrel and annotated lyrics might provide insight into early songwriters' inspiration and provide youngsters groundwork for writing their own ballads and folk songs.

FRONTIER FAIR

Even though Westerns are out of style these days, or perhaps just for that reason, today's children are fascinated by the lifestyles of the brave and pioneering. Names like Daniel Boone, Davy Crockett, and Annie Oakley may not be as familiar to our children as they were to us—how many of you can sing along with Disney's "Davy, Davy Crockett, king of the wild frontier"?—but such heroes are still folk legends to our children. We may profit from the fact they are not fodder for Saturday morning cartoons anymore, so that the study of their real-life adventures can be a source of interest and admiration to today's child.

Traditional Party

Snacks appropriate to the frontier theme include anything made from apples. Remember Johnny Appleseed: You could plan a whole classroom theme party about this pioneering hero. So bring on the apples; sliced, diced in salad, squeezed into juice or cider, dried as the pioneers preserved them, or baked into cookies and cakes. But hold the icing; frontier households didn't have much sugar! Other appropriate snacks include other dried fruits such as raisins and apricots, granola cereal or bars, oatmeal cookies, gingerbread, spice cakes, honey and biscuits, fruit or meat pies, meat and vegetable stews, venison, or turkey.

ACTIVITIES

Active

Shoe Race. Vary the number of clothing items to be put on according to the age of the children. Have each child run to a "trunk"—cardboard box—and put on pioneer clothes which could include an old work shirt, denim pants or skirt, vest, jacket, hat, boots, belt, or any combination thereof.

Davy, Davy, Daniel, or Pioneer, Pioneer, Indian. Our frontier variations of Duck, Duck, Goose.

Hunt. You might have children go hunting for food for their table—berries or game. Cut appropriate shapes out of construction paper.

Stand-in-line

Pin-the-Tail-on-the-Donkey. It works just fine all by itself for this theme or you could pin the tail on the ox, or pin the yoke on the ox, or pin the wheel on the Conestoga wagon.

Quiet

Shapes and straws. Use wagon wheels—circles with spokes drawn on them—turkeys, sunbonnets, or "berries"—circles of red, purple or black cut in shapes.

Lotto. Your symbols could include bonnets, fur skins, wagons, trunks, barrels, animal shapes, cabins, trees, and apples.

Read a story—about Johnny Appleseed, Davy Crockett, Daniel Boone, Annie Oakley, or a chapter of a Laura Ingalls Wilder book.

Watch a filmstrip or movie. Check the library or video store.

Extended Party

There are many, many crafts of this period that could be learned at an extended Frontier Fair party. All of them require some assistance from expert hands, so we recommend only attempting one such craft at an extended party. Either recruit an expert at one of these crafts or read up on the techniques in a craft book and practice at home before attempting to teach children any of the following skills. Tin punching on jar lids, candle dipping, knot tying, rope making, corn-husk-doll construction are all frontier skills that can be taught to children. (Remember that Melinda learned to make corn-husk dolls one day and taught fifth-graders to do it the next. If she can do it, you can too!)

Cooking projects are fun for the extended day party. You might bake an apple pie, make applesauce, bake bread, make biscuits, churn butter, or prepare stew.

Stations could be arranged at which children could design their own quilt patterns with construction paper, study maps of their area as they would have looked in this time period and trace the frontier trails, build Conestoga wagons from construction paper and tag-board, or make a frontier vest from a paper bag.

Again, students may want to act out a skit from a reading book based on real historical events or play the characters in a story you read aloud.

You may read or tell them a legend from the time period—about Paul Bunyan, Johnny Appleseed, or Pecos Bill. They could act it out or write their own tall tale. You might do an add-a-line tale in which each child adds a line to a class story. You could do this on paper, or sit around the "campfire" or the "hearth" and tell the tale aloud as folks would have done long ago.

Do a little research on the history of your own geographical area. Are there any folk heroes of this time period from your town? Any legends built up about the founders of your town? Did any of the folk heroes we all know wander in your geographic territory? Your area could be a rich source of material.

Long-Term Project

There are many learning opportunities in a theme based on the days of the pioneer. Research topics relevant to this theme include folklore, trails, costumes, food, transportation, backgrounds, religion, and aspirations of the pioneers; Indian tribes; relationships of pioneers to Indians; the Hollywood view of frontierspeople versus reality; or any one of the many frontier heroes.

One group project that might be a very revealing learning experience for the kids would be for them to make a life-sized "covered wagon." They don't need to build an actual wagon; just to measure an area representing the size of a real wagon and mark it off on the floor with tape or blankets. This physical representation of the space in which pioneers lived and carried all their worldly goods for six months should amaze the children. Then let them fill their wagons with the things the average pioneer took on the trip west: trunks, boxes, barrels, furniture. Let them research what the necessities for such a trip were, what household items would be nice to have, what luxuries some folks tried to transport. Let them make group decisions about what they would take with them.

Another way to approach this long-term project would be to plan a Frontier Fair as the culminating event of a month-long study unit. After a month of research and study, fair day could be celebrated with all members of the class, staff, and volunteers coming to school in costume and attending a fair at which any number of craftspeople present their skills and perhaps teach them to the children; a special feast is prepared; a play presented; and stories, reports, and projects presented and shared. The day could include any one or a combination of the above.

A number of field trips would be appropriate. A trip to an old graveyard may reveal much about the life spans of the frontiersman and woman, their religious and philosophical beliefs, their families, and their hardships. You might want to teach the children how to take rubbings from gravestones. There may be an old pioneer trail in your area that students could visit and follow. Perhaps they could take a four-mile hike along such a trail; four miles is what the pioneer wagon averaged per day! There might be in your area, as there is in ours, a pioneer village home that preserves a clear representation of the home life of the pioneer settler.

Very young children might enjoy a "camping" trip right in their own classroom, as they do in teacher Patti Kacere's kindergarten classes every year. Keep in mind that a long-term project for this age child means a week-long program at most. During that week, let the kids color a forest of shelf-paper trees that you hang from the ceiling, read stories about pioneers traveling west and their camping out every night, discuss appropriate clothing for a camp out, plan a camp-out menu. The day before the camp out, erect pop-up tents in the middle of the room. On the day itself, cook stew over a gas stove, have drinks in a cooler, bring sandwiches, and eat picnic style. Let the kids make beds of blankets or sleeping bags in tents and take turns napping. Read stories about camping out, sing camp songs, pretend to go fishing, hunting, canoeing, boating, swimming, and so on.

An interesting idea for a bulletin board might be to put up a map of the United States and pretend your class is embarking on the trip west. Choose your starting point—perhaps your own hometown if appropriate or an historical starting point—and your destination—again maybe your city or some city west of the Rockies. Each day, mark your progress. Discuss the challenges you might have met today—crossing a river, traveling over mountains, hitting bad weather, encountering Indians. Discuss how you would deal with disease, boredom, exhaustion, food preparation, water supplies, and injuries to people and animals.

The frontier theme ties in or overlaps with such historical issues as the Revolutionary War, the Civil war, immigrants, cowboys, native Americans, the gold rush in California and Alaska, the Texan War of Independence, the growth of lumbering and other industries, the Wild West, and many other topics of interest. It seems clear that such a theme can inspire an infinite number of research areas and resource possibilities.

We hope you have been inspired by our suggestions for these three historical themes and have seen even more possibilities in each of the ideas. In case you are looking for more ideas of an historical nature, the following are a few topics on which you might want to brainstorm and create your own very special theme parties.

OTHER HISTORICAL THEMES

May Day. From honoring the Roman goddess Flora to Maid Marian's cohorts dancing around the Maypole in merry olde England to the Soviets marching in Red Square in modern times, May Day is definitely a great day around which to build an historical theme party.

Mythology. Melinda's mother still has the elementary reader in which she, at six and seven, learned all about the legendary creatures and gods worshipped by the ancient Greeks and Romans. How many children today can even name one such god or goddess—unless we've named a planet after it? Surely these ancient legends so rich in romance and adventure are great study and party theme material for creative and curious young minds.

Roman holiday. We're not recommending a toga party in the tradition of *Animal House*, but we do see endless possibilities in the concept of a Roman banquet party. Peel me a grape, Calpurnia!

Recent history. How much do your kids really know about World War II or the sizzlin' sixties? Do they know the names Eisenhower and Lindbergh? Pick a decade since the 1900s and build a theme around America in that time. You have plenty of living resources right in your own backyard.

RESOURCES

Aliki. *A Medieval Feast.* New York: Thomas Y. Crowell, 1983.

Dinosaurs! Supplement to *Childcraft: The How and Why Library.* Chicago, Ill.: World Book, Childcraft International, Inc., 1987.

Hall, Donald. *Ox Cart Man.* Children's Choice: Scholastic Book Services. New York: Viking Press, 1979.

Macaulay, David. *Castle.* Boston: Houghton Mifflin, 1977.

Rutland, Jonathon. *Knights and Castles.* New York: Random House, 1987.

9 We're Not Talking Yogurt

Cultural Parties

To quote that most infuriating song, the mere mention of which will have you humming it in your head all day, "It's a small, small world." Trite, but true. One lesson we must not fail to teach our children in this age of nuclear power and environmental threats is that we are all our brothers' keepers; that if we are to keep the planet Earth in working order, we are all going to have to pull together. As citizens of the world, we must all learn to get along with our neighbors—the neighbors on the street where we live, the neighbors in our fellow cities and states, and the neighbors across our borders and across the seas. To foster better understanding between the varying cultures in our country and towns and between the countries of the world, we must instill in our children understanding and respect for people of all races, religions, and cultures.

We can teach them that it is O.K. to say that people are different and to study those differences as long as different doesn't mean better or worse or smarter or dumber, just different. We don't all have to share a religion or philosophy or history in order to respect each other. It is more often the case that as we learn about differences between our culture and others, we also discover the similarities in all cultures: This one's religion may have a different name or a different deity but the basic premises of good and evil remain the same; that one's folk heroes may have different legends, but their virtues and their vices are the same. We, as parents, would like to encourage schools to incorporate such teachings into the curriculum as early as possible; we learn best what we learn first.

As volunteers, we can support the enrichment process through the simple introduction of cultural appreciation at classroom parties. Unfortunately, any superficial study of other cultures tends to lure us into the trap of stereotyping. We do not want to leave children with inaccurate images of all Oriental women in kimonos or all Irish people believing in leprechauns; rather, we intend to teach respect for differing traditions and an appreciation of the universality of human nature by examining the lifestyles, the legends, and the lore of our neighbors near and far.

We will now step off our soap box and get right down to some practical suggestions about producing fun, interesting parties around cultural themes. We will highlight the themes of Native Americans, a trip to the Orient, a Mexican Fiesta, and Irish Eyes, and suggest a number of other cultures appropriate for adaptation.

NATIVE AMERICANS

The terms *native American* and *American Indian* are generic, covering numerous separate and distinct cultures. There are Woodland Indians, Plains Indians, Northwest Coastal Indians, Southwest Pueblo Indians, and many groups that started one place and ended in another. In each of those categories are many separate tribes, each of which may have had distinct habits and traditions. It would, of course, be impossible to do justice to each of these separate cultures, and lumping them all together tends to scream of stereotyping, so in a certain sense this theme catches us between a rock and a hard place. Still we feel the study of native Americans is an important pursuit; we feel there are ways to walk the fine line between reinforcing the invalid and potentially damaging cigar-store Indian image and the overwhelming task of trying to fairly represent each and every tribe. While native American cultures are as diverse as the modern American cultures, there are commonalities that apply to native Americans just as there are to Americans in general.

One of the ways to avoid overgeneralization is to focus your party on a particular tribe of Indians that may have inhabited your particular part of the country. For resources about such tribes, contact your local historical museum or society and check at your library. For generalized information about Indians, check with your nearest Boy Scout leader.

Traditional Party

Snacks at a party honoring native Americans must certainly feature corn. Corn chips, corn bread, corn on the cob, creamed corn, plain corn, corn muffins, popcorn, corn tortillas—all fit the theme. Other suitable choices include beef stew, jerky, fresh bread, and fresh apples, pears, and/or other fresh fruit native to the United States.

The type of costume you and/or the children wear can vary depending on the type of Indian on which you are focusing. Generically moccasins, leather clothing, vests, leggings, parkas, feathers, and headpieces all have Indian origins.

ACTIVITIES

Quiet

Sand painting. Three various methods follow.

1. Tint white sand different colors by mixing it with a little dry tempera paint. Make a design on a paper and choose color for each area. Paint glue on each area and sprinkle with colored sand. A squeeze bottle for ketchup or mustard works well to hold sand; just mark the color on outside of each container.

2. Same as above except instead of using tinted sand, use paprika, salt, and pepper.

3. Color with chalk on fine-grained sandpaper.

Make masks. Use paper plates as a base for simulated wooden masks. Brown grocery bags may also be used to resemble a Kachina-style mask. Decorate to taste with markers, crayons, construction paper, feathers, and beads. (Lunch bags may be used for snouts for the paper bag masks.)

Make a miniature shield. Using a three-inch round of cardboard or ends of juice cans, decorate shields with color and/or feathers.

String beads. Using tinted macaroni—color macaroni by quickly dipping it into food coloring and spreading it out to dry—children can string beads onto straws or string to make necklaces or breast plates.

Make a vest. Slit a grocery bag down the front, cut out a neck hole and two arm holes, and let children color, paint, and decorate.

Shapes and straws. Use shapes of teepee, peace pipe, arrowhead, igloos (white half-circles), or feather.

Lotto. Use above shapes and add pueblos (brown squares), totem poles, moccasins, hatchet, eagle, or sun.

Stand-in-line

"Spear" toss. Using a bean bag for a spear or a suction-cup-tipped dart, have children toss "spear" at target of deer or buffalo. Or paint the shape of a deer or buffalo on a board with a hole cut out of the middle. The point is to "spear" the animal by having bean bag go through hole.

Pin-the-Feather-on-the-Headdress. Use a real feather backed with tape. Or Pin-the-Face-on-the-Totem-Pole.

Shoe race. Have kids race to put on vest, moccasins, headdress, bow and arrow, or any combination of these.

Active

Dance. Many simple Indian dance steps can be learned quickly. The toe-heel step is self-explanatory. Let kids practice that to Indian music. Try teaching the circle step next. Let children form a circle and then glide sideways as smoothly as possible. The canoe step sounds fun and is easy. Just point the toe and tap it on the ground three times, then step—tap, tap, tap, step—repeat with the opposite foot. Turn on the Indian music and let them choreograph themselves!

Sioux, Sioux, Apache, or Chief, Chief, Geronimo are variations on Duck, Duck, Goose which familiarize kids with famous Indian names. Substitute any tribe or chief names that might be more appropriate in your area.

Extended Party

For a longer party, let the crafts we described earlier become more extensive, larger, and more detailed. Let the kids really spend some time with their creations.

In addition, children at a longer party might have time to do a few more complicated crafts. Many little boys—and girls—will get a kick out of decorating their own shields. Using ten-inch circles of wood, cardboard, or papier-mâché to which you have stapled or securely glued two cloth loops to the back for arm and hand, let children paint Indian designs and add feather decorations.

Indians used totem poles to tell stories or to tell something about the person who put them up. Totem poles might brag about an individual's family or make fun of an enemy. Story-telling totem poles illustrated the important moments in a story. Creating totem poles, especially after children learn what Indians used them for, becomes a fascinating activity. Use styrofoam cups, salt or cocoa boxes, or any small container that can be stacked for the body of the pole. Separate each level with an index card. Children can decorate each section with paint and/or construction paper to create their own poles. Larger poles may be constructed of oatmeal boxes.

Constructing models of native American homes is also a viable project at an extended day party. For example, use sugar cubes to build igloos; cloth or leather and sticks for teepees; and boxes, papier-mâché, and/or clay to make pueblos.

Many stick-and-ball games that are popular today are based on very similar native American games; one example is lacrosse. If you have the space and the time, try teaching the children the basics of one of these.

Long-Term Project

There are a number of large projects that lend themselves to this theme. Building life-size teepees or wigwams, constructing realistic pieces of native costumes, making realistic jewelry, studying the art of archery, and/or studying and emulating the lifestyle of a particular tribe are some group or class projects that come immediately to mind. Each of these projects would require extensive research and planning on the students' part—as well as consideration of such issues as acquiring materials, learning a skill, seeking expert assistance—all of which are areas in which volunteer support can make such projects possible.

Stations featuring any of the activities previously mentioned could be appropriately set up during the weeks of the study. Other stations might be Indian music, featuring tapes as well as real instruments to experiment with; Indian religion, including books explaining the religions and models of or real Indian religious icons; daily life of an Indian child in a particular tribe, with examples of Indian toys and dolls and clothing; and Indian legends, featuring books, filmstrips, or videotapes of dramatic presentations of the legends.

Suitable field trips include excursions to any nearby Indian historical site (mounds, villages, reservations, etc.), an archery range, the local historical museum, or any area art museum featuring Indian art.

Research topics might be an intense study of the habits of one particular tribe, a study of Indian treaties, Indian reservations, the native American in today's society, archery, Indian cooking, gold, Indian religions, the Indian and the frontiersperson and/or pioneer, the Hollywood Indian, biographical study of any one famous native American, and/or a study of the tribes of one geographic area. A class research project might be to pick one tribe and follow its evolution from before the settlers landed in America through modern times. Bulletin boards during this entire unit might feature one particular tribe, a U.S.A. map pinpointing the tribes inhabiting each area during certain time periods, the ecosystem of the early native American, or native American heroes—modern and historical.

The final celebration for this study unit could be a powwow. Each child or groups of children could choose a tribe to represent. On Powwow Day, children could wear appropriate costumes and bring one item—food, clothing, jewelry, art, hunting tool—representative of their tribe that they have made, found, drawn a picture of, or found a photo of to share with the class. A native American feast could be served and the day celebrated with tribal dancing—either by children or special guests.

WHEN IRISH EYES ARE SMILING!

We include the Irish theme not just because it is rich in possibilities, but also because it fits so well with a traditional school-party holiday—St. Patrick's Day. Here's a good place to start introducing the concept of the party as a learning experience and the learning experience as a party.

Begin by telling the students why we associate St. Patrick's Day with Ireland—St. Patrick lived and worked in Ireland centuries ago and became the patron saint of Ireland because of his religious and cultural teachings; why shamrocks are so frequently used as symbols of the day—St. Patrick is said to have used a shamrock to demonstrate the concept of the Holy Trinity; and why green is the symbolic color of Ireland and St. Patrick—because of Ireland's nickname, the Emerald Isle. You may just outright tell these facts to little ones; the discovery of these facts might be one of your quiet games for older children. What we don't want is children walking away from a St. Patrick's Day celebration thinking all Irishmen wear green suits and tall hats, smoke pipes, and believe in leprechauns. So while you are reading a story about leprechauns or leading a round of Pin-the-Pot-of-Gold-to-the-End-of-the-Rainbow, remember to include a few remarks about the fact that these are just folk legends and that Irish people believe in leprechauns the way we believe in Paul Bunyan or the tooth fairy.

Traditional Party

The possibilities for snacks at an Irish party are almost endless. Besides the obvious choice of Irish stew, you can serve anything made from potatoes since potatoes are a staple of the Irish diet and a reminder of the great potato famine and/or anything green, considering what is probably an American mania for dyeing anything and everything green on St. Patrick's Day. Libby Demerly, a volunteer in Lafayette, Indiana, wrote that as her regular volunteer duty, she popped popcorn for sale every Thursday. On St. Patrick's Day, she slipped a little green food coloring into the oil and created a popcorn panic! The kids got so excited about the green popcorn, she not only sold out the popcorn that day, she now has to make it green every Thursday! Luckily the school colors are green and white!

To prepare Irish stew, use any traditional Irish stew recipe you find in your favorite cookbook or simplify your life and cheat: Serve canned stew or make easy stew with ground beef and canned vegetables. Anytime you cheat in a cultural party, though, you must 'fess up. We're trying to avoid stereotyping and misconceptions, but we've also got to work within our time and material constraints and the dietary demands of the kids. It's not much of a party if the snack is not appetizing to the children.

Potato recipes are endless; maybe you could have a potato buffet. Serve such items as traditional potato dishes — baked, mashed, scalloped, fried, au gratin, salad — and potato pancakes, potato pie, potato rolls, potato bread, even potato candy! (To one pound mashed potatoes, add one pound powdered sugar, mix well. Shape into small potato shapes. Roll in a mixture of cinnamon and sugar. Add slivered almond "eyes" if desired. Makes twenty-five to fifty, depending on size. Make ahead or let kids shape and roll their own.)

Every year the kindergartners in Mrs. Fox's class enjoy a St. Patrick's Day green buffet. Notes are sent home asking parents to contribute. The day of the party a feast of green is laid out for children to enjoy — everything from celery sticks to pistachio pudding. Says Mrs. Fox, "In kindergarten, everything is learning." The green buffet reinforces not just color recognition; its diversity of offerings begs for a discussion about a balanced diet. "And," adds Mrs. Fox, "there are fine motor skills involved in feeding on finger foods and balancing a napkin."

ACTIVITIES

Quiet

Shapes and straws. Cut out green shamrocks, black pots, gold bricks, or brown potatoes for shapes.

Fun sheets. Let the little ones color sheets on the Irish theme: a rainbow, for example, or a "big and little" sheet using giants and leprechauns. Older children may work crossword puzzles of Irish facts and legends or word finds of Irish geographic features.

Lotto. Use symbols of shamrock, pot, rainbow, leprechaun, pipe, potato, gold bricks, top hat, or walking stick.

Crafts. Older children might enjoy carving their own stamp out of a potato. Little ones might like to use already-carved potato stamps to create their own designs.

Stand-in-line

Pin-the-Pot-of-Gold-at-the-End-of-the-Rainbow. Draw a big rainbow on poster board; fashion a black pot overflowing with yellow "gold" to be pinned on poster.

Clothespins in the Bottle. Using little wooden people from Fisher-Price or any generic type of action figure or small doll and a shoe or dark-colored bottle, drop the "leprechaun" into the "underground tunnel."

Bean Bag Toss. Using any bean bag or ones you've made specially out of gold fabric, toss the "gold" into the "pot" or at the end of the rainbow.

Active

Hunt. Cut out shamrock shapes or gold bricks or wrap tiny boxes of raisins in gold foil and hide them around the room.

Shamrock, Shamrock, Leprechaun. This party's version of Duck, Duck, Goose.

Musical Chairs variation. While playing an Irish jig have children sitting on floor pass around a cut-out shamrock, a raisin-box "gold brick," or a gold bean bag. The person who holds the "bag" when the music stops is out, and so on.

Dance an Irish jig. You provide the music and let the kids choreograph their own Irish jig. Great for little ones.

To add to the festive spirit, you may come to the party dressed all in green—complete with tall felt hat, pipe, and walking stick, or however the spirit moves you. You might paint a shamrock on willing little cheeks with greasepaint or tempera paint.

Extended Party

You might want to do one of the following fun crafts or set up stations so that children may choose to do one or all of them.

Leprechaun puppets. Using an overturned styrofoam cup as the start for the puppet, children may glue orange yarn around the closed end of the cup for hair, top it with a hat made out of green construction paper, and encircle the wide, open end with a green cloth collar. In the middle, they can draw facial features, and they've built their leprechaun.

Leprechaun ears. Children may fashion their own leprechaun ears to wear at the party or as characters in a story they act out during the party. All they need is a pattern to copy: a teardrop shape about five or six inches long. At the wide end, a circle about three inches in diameter is cut out so that the ear fits over the child's ear. Small children will delight in creating their own ears; older children may enjoy creating a complete costume with construction-paper hat and mustache.

Shamrock cuttings. Buy one or two shamrock plants at your local greenhouse. Provide styrofoam cups and potting soil and have the children propagate plant cuttings so that each can take home a shamrock plant or their own. You might include mimeographed instructions for keeping the plant alive at home (how often to water, how much light it likes, etc.).

Story reading. Read a story about Ireland or by an Irish author. Since Ireland is famous for its poets and writers, perhaps with the help of your librarian you can find a suitable work. You may have children act out parts of the characters while you read.

Long-Term Project

Because of the part rainbows play in Irish folklore, it might be appropriate for the youngest children to focus a whole unit on color recognition around this Irish theme. For each day of the week before the party, have a color day. For example, Monday might be blue day: Everyone should try to wear at least one blue item of clothing, and children might bring one object from home that is traditionally blue—such as a flower, a ballpoint pen, or a picture of a police officer in a blue uniform. During story time, the teacher might read a blue book such as *Blueberries for Sister Sal*. The snack could be color coordinated: blueberry yogurt, blueberries, or blueberry jam on crackers. Now that we've picked the hardest color, you can think of any number of things to do for red, green, yellow, and orange! Naturally, on the big party day, all the colors of the rainbow should be included in every aspect of the party.

Children in first through third grades might want to pick up on the *little* concept of the Irish little people. You can make a bulletin board about all the mythical little people in the world, such as gnomes, fairies, leprechauns, and brownies. All during the unit, children could read "little" books like *Little Red Riding Hood, The Three Little Pigs,* excerpts from *Little House on the Prairie* and *Little Women* or little books such as the child-size volumes of Beatrix Potter or Lois Lensky. Children could write "little" stories of their own about little, mythical creatures, using little in their titles, or writing on little books made from cut paper. Math activities could center around the concepts of smaller than and greater than, graphs, ratios, and fractions.

Older children could study Ireland's history and culture. Appropriate avenues of research would include myths and folklore, religious conflict, the potato famine, the Irish immigrant in America, peat and peat bogs, and Irish poets and writers.

Some stations that could be set up include a musical station featuring tapes of Irish folk songs, a literature station including excerpts of poetry and prose written by Irish authors and perhaps some tapes of this literature being read aloud, a pen-pal station where children could write to Irish schoolchildren of their own age, and a potato cookbook station where students could research and share potato recipes for a class cookbook. You might like to make the latter a tasting station and have students bring samples of their recipes to be judged by class members.

MEXICAN FIESTA

Mexico is one of our nearest neighbors, yet for many of our elementary students, particularly those living outside of the Southwest, Mexico is little more than a name. Beyond appreciating the bright colors of the Mexican sombrero they've seen hanging in their favorite Mexican fast-food restaurant, too many of our children know only stereotypes from *Zorro* and a five-minute journey through Disney World's Pirates of the Caribbean. The Mexican Fiesta theme should broaden the scope of our children's knowledge of our southern neighbor—her history, her people, and her traditions.

Traditional Party

If you own or have access to authentic Mexican clothing and/or decorations, use them in every way you can. If you have none or what you have needs supplementation, just use a variety of bright colors—turquoise, red, yellow, green, purple—in your clothing and paper products to give a Mexican flavor to your celebration. Wear lightweight, easy clothes (a loose, peasant blouse and full skirt for the women, all white shirt and trousers for men), sandals, and a splash of turquoise or gold jewelry. If you have working knowledge of Spanish, use it and ask the children to join you: Greet them with buenos dias, call the food by its Mexican name, refer to the party as a fiesta, and so on.

Thanks to the Mexican food rage in the United States today, you will probably not be at a loss for ideas for snacks at this party. You can serve taco chips and bean dip, tacos, nachos, or even sopaipillas—fried biscuit dough—or bunuelos—similar to Apple Grandes served at your favorite Mexican fast-food restaurant. Check any Mexican cookbook for a variety of good finger foods, but for young children go easy on the hot chilies. Chocolate, especially in the form of hot cocoa, is a favorite in Mexico.

ACTIVITIES

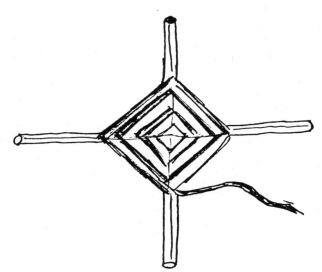

Quiet

Craft. Make ojos de dios (God's eyes), simple wall hangings made from straws and yarn. Cross two popsicle sticks or straws. Wrap variegated yarn around a stick and weave it to the next. Repeat so that yarn design spirals outward from inner cross.

Craft. Paint or stencil a floor tile. Using bright acrylic paints, let children draw or stencil traditional Mexican designs on a floor tile. Check your library and/or craft store for design patterns. Adding circles of felt to the bottom of these tiles makes them into great trivets.

Craft. Stringing bright beads into bracelets, necklaces, or hat bands is a great craft for little ones.

Craft. Make paper flowers from tissue paper or coffee filters.

Shapes and straws. Cut shapes of sombreros, maracas, or serapes.

Stand-in-line

Break the piñata. Hang a Mexican piñata from the ceiling and let the children take turns being blindfolded and trying to hit the piñata with a long stick.

Pin-the-Tail-on-the-Donkey. Since the burro is a common part of Mexican rural life, no adaptation is necessary for this game.

Shoe race. This game is particularly fun if you have authentic Mexican clothes—a sombrero, serape, peasant blouse, skirt, or dress that they can take turns putting on and taking off.

Active

Dance. Play Mexican music and let children do a Mexican hat dance.

Musical chairs. Play the traditional game using Mexican music.

Pato, Pato, Ganso. This is Duck, Duck, Goose in Spanish!

Extended Party

More extensive projects for an extended party would include a number of craft activities. Children of any age might enjoy creating a class mural. Using sidewalk chalk and drawing on the sidewalk or playground outside or chalk and/or tempera paint on rolls of brown paper, let children create a Mexican scene. Some thinking ahead is necessary here; children need to learn about the Mexican people, their lifestyle, and the countryside by looking at picture books and encyclopedias. They need to get a feel for the colors and styles of their art and folk art in the same manner. Books offering such insights could be made available at stations which children could visit during the day or week before the party; or during the party, groups of children could each study one particular book and then share ideas before they begin the work. For younger children, it might speed things up to have a basic outline drawn on the mural paper, and let them color in the scene.

Similarly, children might have time to make simple piñatas at an extended party. Cover inflated balloons with papier-mâché, let them dry for two days, then decorate with crepe paper and bright paints. You might have to divide children into groups and let each group create one piñata. To save time at the party, you might have already done the papier-mâché step and just let the children decorate their piñatas.

Other activities for an extended party are to have lessons in Spanish and see if children can carry on simple conversations. Examining the currency of a foreign country is always interesting, so if you have Mexican coins and/or bills, bring them to class.

Finally, watching a movie or filmstrip about Mexico or Mexican Americans, reading a story and/or acting out a story about Mexico or a Mexican folktale are all fun activities.

Long-Term Project

Probably the most enjoyable large project on Mexico would be to plan a fiesta celebrating the studies of the class. Children could set up a market and sell the Mexican wares they have produced—decorated terra-cotta flowerpots, any sort of pots or vases fashioned from clay, tissue paper flowers, ojos de dios, and all kinds of Mexican foods. If you can, use real pesos for currency, or make fake pesos ahead of time. Have all the wares and foods labeled in Spanish and encourage the children to speak Spanish as much as they can. After the market, have a feast of Mexican foods and play Mexican music and dance.

There are many possible stations. A musical one could feature a guitar, Mexican guitar music, and tapes of Mexican guitar playing. An Alamo station could include books about the battle, biographies of some of our famous frontierspeople who gave their lives there, a biography of the victorious Mexican general, and perhaps a filmstrip on the topic. Another might focus on the plight of the Mexican economy and/or the life of the Mexican migrant worker. Children might be the focus of one—their schooling, their average home life, the kinds of games and sports they enjoy, their heroes, and so on. Folk art and culture might be another topic: Collect whatever artifacts you and/or other resource people might be able to share, and display these along with books or *National Geographic* featuring photographs and articles about Mexican arts and crafts.

Fun and fascinating group projects include building a model of the Alamo, taking an imaginary trip through Mexico and discussing each stop along your journey, building a model Aztec settlement, or adopting or studying a parrot. Appropriate research topics would include any of the Indian cultures of Mexico (e.g., Aztecs, Mayans), some famous Mexicans (e.g., Cortez, Pizarro, Montezuma), Mexican holidays, Indian ruins, Mexican agriculture and industry, life in the cities, life in rural areas, and Mexico's tourist industry.

Check out your community for interesting guest speakers: any Mexican Americans, anyone who has visited Mexico and can share slides or photos, anyone who has studied in Mexico, a high school Spanish teacher, a Mexican exchange student or college student, an anthropologist or a college professor expert in Mexican cultures.

A TRIP TO THE ORIENT

A rapidly changing aspect of U.S. foreign policy in the past few decades has been the relationship with our oriental neighbors. Only a few years ago, we had no diplomatic relations with China and our cultural relations with Japan were often limited to making fun of any product with the label "Made in Japan." Times have certainly changed, and to keep up with these new relationships we think it appropriate that children of all ages be exposed to the cultures and traditions of the Orient.

To simplify the short-term party plans, we have kept the title of this section generic—instead of restricting ourselves to just one country. We feel justified in doing so because the Far Eastern cultures, like the countries of Eastern Europe, share some basic traditions: With some slight variations, their traditional native costumes are similar; their religions similar in tenet and tone; their diets based on the same types of food and preparations; their family structures alike; and their cultural offerings of music, art, and theater have similar styles and subject matter. That is not to say that China, Japan, Korea, and their neighbors do not have separate and unique cultures; that is to say that as with all the countries of South America or both the United States and Canada, some generalities about these cultures can be made.

By generalizing these cultures, then, it is possible to hold a traditional classroom party at which children sit at low tables and sip tea and eat rice and vegetables and fortune cookies without offending any particular culture by serving Korean tea with Japanese traditional vegetables and Chinese cookies. Our purpose rather is to sketch a broad—while still vivid and accurate—outline of the lifestyles of our oriental neighbors. Older children working in long-term projects or at extended parties may examine the differences between individual cultures.

Traditional Party

As we mentioned above, we are traveling to the generic world of the Orient. If you have a silk kimono or anything remotely like one, wear it. Take off your shoes as you enter the room and kneel on the floor to eat. Decorate the room with Japanese lanterns and use oriental shades of paper products—violets, reds, purples, and blues trimmed in gold, and any oriental design or motif.

Snacks can consist of anything made with rice, rice cakes, stir-fried vegetables, fish dishes, egg rolls, almond cookies, fortune cookies, and tea. Check your favorite cookbooks for simple, authentic oriental recipes. Shop at your local oriental grocery for other treats such as Chinese noodles and Japanese candy. Be sure to serve everything with chopsticks.

ACTIVITIES

Quiet

Craft. Origami is the perfect craft for an oriental party. Get a book from the library and teach yourself how to fold a few simple objects, or find a guest expert in origami to come and demonstrate for the children.

Shapes and straws. Cut shapes in the form of fans, parasols, kimonos, pagodas, fish, or flowers.

Lotto. Use all of the shapes included above plus chopsticks, oriental slippers, the Buddha, and outlines of the countries.

Craft. Bring fat paint brushes, black paint or ink, and rice paper as well as a poster illustrating the Chinese or Japanese alphabet and let the children experiment with writing in oriental script.

Stand-in-line

Pin-the-Sash-on-the-Kimono. Use a poster of an oriental girl or draw your own.

Shoe race. Use a bathrobe kimono, sandals, and a rubber band to make a ponytail on every racer's head as the objects to be put on and taken off in the relay race.

Active

Baseball. Since baseball is a national sport in Japan, a game of the "all-American" sport is certainly appropriate here.

Kite flying. Kites originated in the Orient, so what could be more appropriate than the class flying kites on the playground?

Musical cushions. Play Musical Chairs using large cushions.

Fortune, Fortune, Cookie. This is a variation on Duck, Duck, Goose.

Extended Party

When you have more time at an extended party, you might want to limit yourself to just one of the oriental cultures and study it more closely. Authenticate your snacks and prepare the food in the classroom with the children as chefs. Learn how to count to ten and/or say a few elementary phrases in the language and teach it to the class. Invite a guest speaker who has visited the country recently to share his or her experiences and pictures. Find an exchange student from that country to speak to the class. Get a local martial arts expert to give a demonstration in karate, kung fu, or judo. Read and/or act out a story or folktale from that country, or watch a movie or filmstrip about the country.

Long-Term Project

Some appropriate long-term projects are building a volcano; pagoda; typical Japanese, Chinese, or Korean home, or an oriental garden. Students might be interested in studying such topics as flower arranging, volcanos, paper making, origami, raku pottery, oriental cooking, the Japanese electronics industry, the family structures of the Orient, or traditional theaters, music, and art forms. As the resource person, you might be able to locate experts in any of these fields to come speak to the class as a whole or to meet with small groups of students.

OTHER CULTURAL THEMES

Italy. Columbus Day might get a whole new image were you to use it as a springboard for studying the rich cultural history of Italy. Think of Da Vinci, Michelangelo, the Roman Empire, and Venice; all fascinating, romantic topics for study and celebration.

Oktoberfest. The Germans and the Slavic neighbors have for centuries celebrated the harvest with Oktoberfest, which provides you with a terrific cultural theme party. Think of the food—Wiener schnitzel, bratwurst, sauerkraut, tortes, and strudels. Those dishes are almost as fun to say as they are to eat.

Soviet Union. Take advantage of glasnost if you can and gather as many materials as you can to teach your children about the real life of the people of the Soviet Union. Theirs is a culture rich in tradition and great food, and they are a people of determination and hard work. Knowledge is our best weapon against the distrust and hate we were taught to feel for the Soviets when we were in school.

RESOURCES

The Big Bear Cub Scout Book. Irving, Tex.: Boy Scouts of America, 1984.

Blood, Charles L. *American Indian Games and Crafts.* New York: Franklin Watts, 1981.

Childcraft: The How and Why Library, Vol. 3. Chicago, Ill.: World Book, Childcraft International, Inc., 1981.

The Indian Book: Supplement to *Childcraft: The How and Why Library.* Chicago, Ill.: World Book, Childcraft International, Inc., 1980.

McCloskey, Robert. *Blueberries for Sal.* Children's Choice: Scholastic Book Services. New York: Viking Press, 1948, 1976.

Whiteford, Andrew Hunter, and Zim, Herbert S. *North American Indian Arts.* New York: Golden Press, 1970.

Wolf Cub Scout Book. Irving, Tex.: Boy Scouts of America, 1986.

10 Bookworms Are Party Animals

We can't think of a more valuable way that volunteers can contribute to our schools than by promoting an interest in reading. Why else would Traci spend so much of her time at area schools and libraries dressed in a red furry jumpsuit or Melinda try to negotiate her stick shift wearing a hoop skirt? We transform ourselves into Clifford and Mother Goose—and the Owl's pussycat and one of Shel Silverstein's kids and Tom Sawyer and Garfield—in order to communicate to children the sense of magic reading can bring. We want to show that even grown-ups, as well as kids, can find romance, fun, adventure, and learning in books.

Besides sponsoring the special events focused on reading as outlined in chapter 14 and/or rewarding and emphasizing reading through various classroom activities as mentioned in chapter 12, hosting a classroom party using a specific book as a theme is a festive, fun way to reinforce the idea that reading is important. It is also a particularly effective way to transform just another classroom sugar binge into a party with a purpose!

NURSERY RHYMES

Obviously this theme would be most appropriate for pre-kindergarteners through first-graders. There is, however, much about life in the eighteenth and nineteenth centuries in Western Europe, Great Britain,

and the early American colonies that can be learned by studying the facts surrounding and the folklore illustrated by Mother Goose's famous verses. In fact, Melinda has presented such minilessons in Mother Goose to children in grades up to four. The kids really enjoyed seeing another side to the familiar rhymes. The "scholarly" study of Mother Goose gave those older children the opportunity to both feel adult by looking back with a superior air at the rhymes of their babyhood and to indulge the part of them that still enjoyed listening and repeating the rhymes.

Traditional Party

If you'd like, as host or hostess of this party, you could come dressed as Mother Goose or as any one of her many familiar characters. Appropriate snacks include cookie shapes (mittens, eggs, cats, crowns, flowers, etc.), tarts, pies, hot cross buns, muffins of any sort, homemade breads, cucumber sandwiches, beef or chicken broth, stew, soups, cottage cheese, milk, tea, or apple juice.

Those who enjoy baking and cake decorating could make the following Jack-and-Jill cake. Decorate a layer cake or sheet cake with green icing and green-colored coconut—grass. Use a cupcake iced in chocolate as a well in the middle of the cake. A gingerbread boy and girl or animal-cracker people serve as Jack and Jill and a gumdrop is the pail.

ACTIVITIES

Quiet

Craft. Make a crown for Old King Cole or the Queen of Hearts. Cut strips of construction or typing paper with zigzag points on one long edge. Let children decorate their crowns with crayons, markers, ribbons, sequins, or craft-store jewels. Then tape the ends of each crown to fit the child's head.

Fun sheets. Color pictures of nursery rhyme characters. These may be used as place mats. For older kids, use word finds, crossword puzzles, color graphs, or have children create their own illustrations for familiar rhymes.

Write a rhyme. Together the class or small groups of children can make up a rhyme while the leader writes the dictated verses on a blackboard or flip sheet. Children might each want to draw a picture to go with rhymes.

Rhyme games. The leader suggests a word, and children come up with rhyming words. Perhaps the leader can write lists of rhyming words on a blackboard or flip sheet.

Read aloud. Read children's favorites aloud. Let kids act one—"Little Miss Muffet" is good. Let children create with you. Share several different Mother Goose books with the same rhymes but different illustrations, or discuss some rhymes that have a number of common variations. Or read one long verse such as "Old Mother Hubbard," with which kids are probably only familiar with the first couple of verses. For older children, read some rhymes they've never heard before.

Puzzle. Cut egg shapes into puzzles and have them put Humpty Dumpty back together again.

Stand-in-line

Clothespins in the bottle. Use little wooden people and drop them in an old shoe or boot of Dad's.

Pin-the-Apron-on-Bo-Peep or **Pin-the-Sheep** (cotton balls with masking tape on back) **-in-the-Pasture** or **Pin-the-Bandage-on-Jack's-Head.** Variations on this game are endless.

Shoe race. Use an old shoe for "The Old Woman Who Lived in a Shoe" or use an apron and chef's hat for "Hot Cross Buns" or put a penny in a pocketbook for "Lucy Locket."

Active

Songs. "Ring around the Rosie," "London Bridge," "Here We Go Round the Mulberry Bush," or "Pat-a-Cake."

Jack Be Nimble contest. Have a broad jump and/or high jump contest on the playground or in the gym.

Jack, Jack, Jill, or **Tuffet, Tuffet, Spider.** Variations on Duck, Duck, Goose.

Extended Party

It might be fun at an extended party to have a Mother Goose buffet and include many of the foods mentioned in the nursery rhymes. Children also might help prepare the food. You could bake bread, a pie, hot cross buns, and others; decorate cookies in shapes; or let very little ones make their bakeshop goodies out of peanut butter playdough.

Stations of activities listed above could be set up at an extended party so that children could make a hat and a place mat, draw a picture, look at several different Mother Goose books, and write their own rhymes.

The acting out of nursery rhymes could be more of a production. Perhaps the class could be divided into three or four small groups—as long as there's one adult to supervise each group—and each group could work on acting out one rhyme. Then each group could present their verse to the whole class. Simple costumes or props could be included in such productions—paper crowns, aprons, pretend food, stuffed animals, kitchenware, and so on.

A cute idea for a hunt for this party is to have children find Bo Peep's lost sheep. Cotton balls hidden around classroom are the sheep. Glue cotton balls onto tiny packs of raisins and the children can find their treat!

Long-Term Project

As we mentioned for the small children—who would possibly be participating in this theme—*long term* means a week. Every day during the week, a certain time could be "Rhyme Time." You could come in each day and read a different nursery rhyme or teach them all a new rhyme. You could also play a round of rhyming words or a variation in which children find all things in the room that rhyme with a certain word.

Another way to focus attention on Mother Goose rhymes during the week would be to have each day center on a different rhyme. For example, Monday could be "Bo Peep/Little Boy Blue" Day. In the morning read the rhyme. At snack time, have them find the raisin sheep which you have hidden before school. Bring a stuffed sheep and place it prominently in the room. Talk about sheep at circle time. At recess or play time, have a relay race carrying a cotton ball on a spoon.

Tuesday could be "Old Woman in the Shoe" Day: Read the rhyme, bring a variety of shoes for display, practice shoe-tying skills, play the shoe race or clothespins in the bottle, and for the snack serve broth and buttered bread.

Declare Wednesday "Humpty Dumpty" Day. Eat egg salad for the snack, do Humpty Dumpty puzzles from pictures of Humpty that kids have colored, and talk about riddles and tell other riddles. At recess play toss and pretend the ball or bean bag is an egg.

Let Miss Muffet be Queen of Thursday. Make paper spiders using construction paper for the bodies and string for legs. You might want to hang these from the ceiling. Bring a stool for a tuffet corner where children can retreat to look at Mother Goose books. Serve cottage cheese for the snack, and at recess play spider tag.

And Friday is Party Day!

Does this sound like you'll be spending all morning every day of the week at school? Don't panic! As a volunteer, you need to set up the day, organize the materials, and perhaps be at school to read the rhyme or play a game for ten minutes each morning. But as long as you have provided the creative ideas and made the resources available, the teacher and aides can certainly handle incorporating these activities into their daily routine. You don't have to be there every minute of the week.

If presented in the right manner, the Mother Goose theme is rich in possibilities for older children. If children think they're being talked down to or being forced to do baby work, they won't like this at all. If they consider themselves superior to the rhymes but not to the children that enjoy them or the folklore that surrounds them, they might get a kick out of a project like this. Try studying Mother Goose as a reflection of history, a representative of children's literature, one of the longest lasting and most successful teaching modes, a sociological barometer of the past, and/or a popular childhood staple of generation upon generation. Why have these verses been so well known for so long? What about them makes them so appealing to so many people of so many countries and so many eras?

If you can whet the intellectual appetites of the kids this way, then the door is opened to a variety of study approaches. Kids could interview senior citizens about their memories of nursery rhymes. They could locate and study old volumes of Mother Goose rhymes, trying to see if they can get a representative book from every generation since the turn of the century. They could compare and contrast the rhymes and the illustrations. They could prepare rather elaborate costumes, props, and sets to act out several nursery rhymes for the little kids. There are any number of fascinating research topics suggested by Mother Goose. Is "Ring around the Rosie" really about the plague, for example? What is a sixence or a farthing? What do Little Jack Horner and a king's messenger have in common? Would a pie of four and twenty blackbirds really have been a taste treat for a king in those times? What is a stile, crooked or otherwise? Children could compile an illustrated Mother Goose dictionary, prepare a catalogue of toys for Mother Goose Ltd., make models of the Tower of London, design clothes for Little Bo Peep, and so on.

THROUGH THE LOOKING GLASS

Who could be richer in imaginative party ideas than Mother Goose? What one volume or writer has created more colorful, funnier, more diverse, or more familiar characters? Only Lewis Carroll comes close. Combining his books *Alice's Adventure in Wonderland* and *Through the Looking Glass* provides much rich material for party themes. You may use any one of the great characters from the books as your focus: The White Rabbit could direct you to an emphasis on *late* or telling time, the Mad Hatter could lead you into a hat party, the Queen of Hearts could focus on colors, and so on. You may have a simple, straightforward tea party, or a "mad" tea party where everything is silly. You might want to direct your theme solely to the mirror idea and make everything backward. Other motifs suggest other tangents—odd animals, games like chess, croquet, and cards, big and little, and others.

Traditional Party

The treats should fit into a tea party and/or include the "mad" or backward idea: finger sandwiches, individual cakes, scones, muffins, tarts, pineapple *upside*-down cake for the backwardness, and tea or lemonade served from a teapot. As a hostess, you might want to dress like Alice in a blue dress, Mary Janes, and a white apron. Or for hosts or less ambitious hostesses, a large hat with a price tag transforms you into the Mad Hatter, anything all red or all white works, or wear everything wrong side out and backward.

ACTIVITIES

Quiet

Shapes and straws. Use red or white hearts, diamonds, clubs, or spades, or teapots.

Lotto. Use above symbols as well as card shapes, rabbits, clocks, hats, mushrooms, and roses.

Read "Jabberwocky" aloud to the children, then let them try their hand at drawing a bandersnatch, a jabberwock, or even a slithy tove!

Paint the roses. Any painting project that involves using large amounts of red paint. Painting or coloring things red that aren't meant to be red—trees, zebras, penguins—is a good idea.

Mirror. Have partners stand facing each other. One is looking in the mirror, the other is the partner's image and must do as the "real" person does. Then switch roles.

Memory. You can use the commercial games of this name or a simple deck of regular playing cards to play this old standby.

House of cards. Use the playing cards to construct a building.

Chess, checkers, or any card game for older folks.

Stand-in-line

Pin-the-Watch-on-the-Rabbit or **Pin-the-Caterpillar** (a pipecleaner)**-on-the-Mushroom.**

Shoe race. Use a big white apron, an oversized hat, or a crown and scepter. Or have a shirt and tie and coat to be put on wrong side out and backward.

Active

Musical chairs. Play it backward: March around chairs in silence, and find a seat when the music starts.

Tweedle, Tweedle, Dum. This is a Duck, Duck, Goose variation.

Tweedle Dee race. Do a three-legged race.

Extended Party

At a longer party, stations could feature a variety of card games; lessons in chess, copies of both books to page through, including original versions and any of the many later versions, especially Disney; tapes of readings from the books; a filmstrip or short film based on the books; food preparation for the tea party; paper on which to draw pictures of different characters in the books; mirror writing; and/or fun sheets based on the characters or stories.

You could read aloud a section of the books—"Jabberwocky" or "The Walrus and the Carpenter." Children could devise dramatic interpretations to act while you read or could draw illustrations of one scene. Or read just the lines " 'The time has come', the Walrus said, 'To talk of many things: Of shoes—and ships—and sealing-wax—Of cabbages—and kings...'." Then as a class, as a group, or individually, make lists of a variety of things in the world that interest us.

You could lead a whole exercise discussing dreams and why we have them and what they might mean. Compare how many of us have dreamed of falling, being bigger or smaller than we are, or being in a strange and yet familiar place. Children could write stories or draw pictures about their dreams.

Using the "Jabberwocky" as a model, children could write their own nonsense poems, either individually or as a group. Or the class could just make up a list of crazy words and try writing stories or poems using them. Or groups could make up word lists and challenge other groups to define them.

Long-Term Project

Our first suggestion is to familiarize the children with the stories. Set aside a time each day during which these books are read aloud to the class. After they've become acquainted with the written versions, you might want to expose the children to some of the records and movies based on these books.

Children as young as second grade can be taught the basics of chess, and a class tournament could be held with matches played each day.

All the stations we mentioned previously could be used over a period of time; set up one or two stations per week and encourage every child to visit each station at least once. Bulletin boards should be decorated appropriate to any number of the motifs mentioned or with a cheshire cat, a court scene, a croquet scene, mirror writing, and others.

Research topics that play off these stories include extinct animals such as the dodo, caterpillars, Lewis Carroll, chess, word origins, other practitioners of word fabrication such as Ogden Nash, clocks, hedgehogs, flamingos, dreams, rabbits, English tea parties, the life of the upper middle-class child in Edwardian England, and hatters and why they are mad. Projects appropriate to this theme would be any diorama depicting a scene from the stories, models of book characters fashioned from papier-mâché or soft sculpture, character puppets, book illustrations, or production of a play based on the story.

The project might culminate in the presentation of the play; individual or group presentation of their projects; an authentic high tea; a backward party in which everyone comes dressed appropriately and during which everything is done backward (greet everyone with "good-bye," say farewell with "hello," clean up first, then eat, then say the Pledge of Allegiance, etc.); a costume party to which everyone comes dressed as their favorite characters in the book; or a coronation banquet. But don't introduce anyone to the food! Remember " 'Pudding, Alice. Alice, pudding,' at which point the food is taken back to the kitchen because one couldn't possibly eat anyone to whom one had been formally introduced!"

MY FAVORITE ANIMAL BOOK

Children, particularly middle elementary students, are enchanted by books that include animals acting like people. Witness the popularity of such examples as the body of work of Beatrix Potter, the Mousekin books, *Charlotte's Web*, and the Bunnicula series. Classics or recent best-sellers, books about animals are undeniably among children's favorites. Rather than specify one particular book, we have chosen here a slightly generic route; the following theme uses not just one specific book for inspiration, but any of the genre. You and/or the teacher may choose one specific book based on class interest and curriculum or you may want to let kids vote for their favorite. Whatever animal book you choose to center your party around, the following suggestions should suit your needs.

Traditional Party

Snacks should be favorite foods of the particular animal you are featuring: cheese and apples for Mousekin, carrots and/or a vegetable tray for Peter Rabbit, anything red—bloody?—for Bunnicula; junk food for the rat in Charlotte's web. For variety, add cookies cut into appropriate shapes or use the concept of small things in a big world. Mousekin's barbells might be two black olives joined with a toothpick, call a brussel's sprout a head of cabbage, dried apricots cut into tiny wedges for carrots. Carry the big-little theme along by using oversized plates and cups and serving tiny food. Use props such as pop bottle banks, thimble wastebaskets, or foot-tall chess pieces.

ACTIVITIES

Quiet

Read the book or parts of it aloud.

Watch a filmstrip based on the book.

Make a group poster for the book like a movie poster ad.

Make spiders as in nursery rhyme party.

In small groups or as a class, **write** your own Mousekin adventure or make up a new animal with distinctive character about which stories could be written.

Fun sheets. Base these on the books or characters. Children could color pictures of the characters.

Stand-in-line

Make a "Web of Life." This is an ecology game. Children stand in a circle and each child chooses a part of the ecology to represent, such as tree, water, bird, worm, fox, deer, or grass. Use a wide variety of elements and both carnivores and herbivores. You, the sunshine, toss a ball of yarn at one of the children representing something that depends on sun for life. You keep hold of the end of the yarn. That child takes hold of yarn and throws ball to another who uses sun for life. The games continue as children next throw yarn to those who represent animals who feed on vegetation, then animals who feed on animals, and so on. As each child takes hold of the yarn and throws the ball to the next step, the web is formed.

Pin-the-Jacket-on-Peter-Rabbit or **Pin-the-Fly-on-Charlotte's-Web.**

Bean Bag Toss. Toss a rabbit (bean bag) into its nest (potato chip can).

Act out the story or part of the story. Let children take parts to pantomime as you read aloud.

Active

Relay race. Use old, oversized clothes for children to don, using whatever clothing fits your animal.

Peter, Peter, Farmer Brown, or **Charlotte, Charlotte, Fly,** or even **Duck, Duck, Goose** for a Beatrix Potter party.

Parade. Be like the characters in Charlotte's Web at the state fair.

Extended Party

With more time at an extended party, children might enjoy making finger puppets or paper bag puppets to represent characters in the book. Perhaps they could use their puppets to act out the story as you read it aloud. Another appropriate activity would be to fashion sculptures of the characters out of soft soap or clay.

Preparing food is a good activity at an extended party. Shaped sugar cookies might be decorated to more closely resemble the character, cheese and crackers cut, bread baked, pies or tarts prepared, and veggies cleaned and cut.

If Hollywood has jumped on the bandwagon of your character's popularity rent the movie and play it on a VCR. *Charlotte's Web* has been made into a charming film. There are a number of Beatrix Potter books animated in film and an excellent docudrama of her life presented on public television last year. Serve popcorn and lemonade, and you have turned an ordinary afternoon into a party.

Long-Term Project

As with the Lewis Carroll theme, the first step in any long-term project on this theme is to familiarize every child with the book or books. Set aside a time during which the stories or parts of the book will be read aloud to the children. Particularly in the case of Beatrix Potter, include information about the author.

Letter writing is a good project for middle-grade students and here's a great place to put those skills in action. If the author is living, children could write letters to him or her and hope to receive replies before the end of the project. In the case of deceased authors, is there another good place to write—a Beatrix Potter Museum in England or the original publishing company? There are many catalogues for which children could send that market merchandise related to book characters—Beatrix Potter, for example, is now the focus of complete shops.

Research topics suggested by this theme include book reports on each of the books written by one author, a biographical study of the author, a report on the real-life habits of the kinds of animal portrayed in the books, a story of the illustrator of the books if different from the author, and/or a study of the ways the animal's behavior reflects human behaviors. Projects suitable to this theme include dioramas; puppets; original, illustrated further adventures of one of the characters; a recipe book for or "by" the character; and models of the character's home or environment.

All of the activities we've mentioned for the traditional party or extended party could apply to the long-term project by either using the station method or by featuring one special activity a day or week or a combination of each. Stations that adapt to this theme include those for listening to audio tapes of the stories being read aloud while children look at the book; examining various copies of the book—different adventures, different characters, or different versions of the same story; doing fun sheets of crossword puzzles, word finds, and so on; doing jigsaw puzzles featuring characters or generic animals of the same type; and blank books—covers made from wallpaper samples, with blank, lined pages sewn inside—for children to write their own further adventures.

The bulletin board and other areas of the room should keep with the theme. Let children sign up for separate committees to take responsibility for such decorating. A field trip to a farm or a zoo or anywhere children could observe the real animals on which the characters are based would be in order.

The culminating event for such a project might be a party to which the character of the book has invited all the children. Perhaps children could take on personae of other characters in the book or other characters created by the same author or even made-up characters that would suit the theme. For example, Peter Rabbit makes invitations and sends them to all his friends: Jemima Puddle Duck, Jeremy Fisher Frog, Mr. McGregor, Flopsy, Mopsy, and Cottontail. Each child in the room becomes one of Peter's friends and on the day of the party comes in costume, a pair of construction paper ears and an apron or overalls. (Making ears and choosing a character and a costume could have been one of the stations earlier in the week.) Peter is the host and the party—definitely a tea party with cucumber sandwiches and carrot cake, don't you think?—centers around the kinds of activities Peter and his friends would have enjoyed.

11 Life's a Jolly Holiday with Volunteers

Holiday parties are by far the most frequent traditional party celebrated in schools; in fact, were you to poll elementary school teachers asking what parties are celebrated in their rooms, we'd bet 99 percent would list Halloween and Valentine's Day as two of their three or four yearly parties. The others would be a year-end celebration and perhaps a winter holiday observation of some sort. Obviously holiday parties are accepted parts of the elementary classroom routine; therefore they offer a perfect opportunity to introduce creative volunteering into your building. This chapter suggests ways to alter the traditional room mother role; to take that rite of baking heart-shaped cookies or pouring "vampire's" punch and transform it into something interesting and valuable as well as fun.

One twist on the traditional holiday theme is to introduce celebrations for lesser-known holidays. Get a calendar that lists lots of holidays, a copy of *The Kid's Diary of 365 Amazing Days* by Randy Harelson, or any one of the books titled *Celebrate Winter, Celebrate Summer,* and so on. (Since these books are designed for use in Christian education, there is a definite religious slant to many activities, but the books are filled with good craft and seasonal ideas as well.) These books will list some kind of observance for every day of the year and plenty of material for unique classroom celebrations.

We have organized this chapter to follow the school calendar, suggesting party ideas for every season and outlining some activities and treats suitable for each theme, but leaving the details to you. We think you've gotten the idea of how to adapt familiar activities and crafts to a theme, how to think creatively in terms of snacks, decorations, and costumes, and how to expand parties from the traditional to an extended party to a long-term project without our having to make step-by-step suggestions. Besides, doing so for every holiday would fill another book!

SEE YOU IN SEPTEMBER

Start the year off on a fun foot with a Labor Day party. While discussing the fact that traditional Labor Day refers to the hard work of our nation's employed adults and offers them a day off from their "labors," you might want to shift the focus of your Labor Day party to the contemplation of all the hard—but fun—work the children, the teacher, and you are going to do together over the year. Keeping with the theme of schoolwork, snacks might be apples, sugar cookies cut and decorated to look like pencils and/or notebooks, or "brain foods" like tuna fish and carrots. You might come dressed as an old-fashioned school marm, and discuss what life was like in a one-room school in the early years of our country. That should help the children appreciate what they have now!

ACTIVITIES

Quiet

Name game. Have whole class or small groups of children sit in a circle. The first child introduces himself or herself and mentions something he or she likes that begins with the same letter as the child's name:

"I'm Traci and I like tulips," for example. The next child repeats the first introduction and adds his or her own, and so on. You might have small children repeat only the introduction of the person immediately before themselves.

Make something for your desk. You could have children decorate a name plate, a juice-can pencil holder, or a homework folder.

Read a story. Read something appropriate to the first week of school. *Mary Had a Little Lamb; The Berenstein Bears Go to School;* a chapter from *Little House on the Prairie, Huckleberry Finn,* or *A Tree Grows in Brooklyn* describing school; or *Miss Switch; Miss Nelson is Missing;* or an excerpt from *Goodbye, Mr. Chips.* There are many, many books from which you could read about schools and teachers.

Stand-in-line

Pin-the-Apple-on-the-Desk or **Pin-the-Book-in-the-Backpack.**

Clothespins in the bottle. Drop the wooden people into the schoolhouse using a decorated shoe box for the schoolhouse.

Active

Work, Work, Rest, or **Pencil, Pencil, Recess.** These are variations on Duck, Duck, Goose.

Musical Chairs. Play "This is the Way We Walk to School" music and race around the desks.

Animal Labor Day. Pretend to be a hardworking animal like a chipmunk or a beaver and pretend to do its work.

Paint the outside of the school building with water.

Mary Poppins. Play music while children work around the room: Arrange their desks, decorate a bulletin board, organize shelves, clean blackboards, and so on.

For an extended party of this kind, just use more than one or two activities. In addition, you might plan a playground picnic for this party and eat the snacks and play the active games outside. It doesn't seem feasible to adapt this theme to a long-term project, since by the time the project ends we'd be into October.

APPLE DAY

Fall is the season of the apple, and there aren't many other fruits around which one could plan a whole party, but apples fill the bill. Beside the obvious field trip to an apple orchard, there are many activities, crafts, legends, and stories that lend themselves to an Apple Day party.

Naturally the snacks must be apples—plain or prepared in any one of the dozens of ways you can come up with. You can dress as elaborately as Johnny Appleseed, simply in overalls as an apple picker, or just put on a little extra blusher and wear your apple cheeks!

ACTIVITIES

Quiet

Apple Cutting. Cut apple crosswise to reveal the star inside. (All our children did this in kindergarten and still occasionally request their apples cut that way!)

Paint apple blossoms. Use a sponge and pink paint to add blossoms to a bare branch drawn in crayon on construction paper.

Make apple blossoms. Decorate a twig by gluing on scrunched-up pink tissue-paper flowers.

Stand-in-line

Pin-the-Apple-on-the-Tree.

Apple piñata. Using a piñata shaped like an apple that you've either made or purchased, let children try to break the piñata and release the goodies inside.

Active

Drop the Handkerchief. Use an apple instead of a handkerchief.

Apple, Apple, Worm. This is a Duck, Duck, Goose variation.

EVERY LITTLE KID'S FAVORITE—HALLOWEEN

There are entire books written about how to give a smashing Halloween party; check your local library. Many of the activities included in these books are appropriate for use in the classroom. Decorating seems to be a great deal of the fun so be sure to include decorations or making a Halloween craft as part of every party.

There is a wide variety of fun snacks for a Halloween party. We recommend that as time permits you let children help prepare these foods. Make spiders from large gumdrops with licorice legs. Decorate cupcakes with orange icing and chocolate-chip or candy-corn features. Serve ghost-shaped cookies with white icing and chocolate-chip eyes. "Monster sandwiches" are rice cakes or round-cut bread with features of parsley, carrot slices, green pepper (etc.) on complexions of cream cheese or peanut butter. Remember that many otherwise reasonable parents tend to send tons of candy on Halloween even though the kids are going trick-or-treating for candy in just a few hours. Why? Who knows. We just suggest that alternatives like the monster sandwiches and veggies and dip—call them vampire teeth and green slime or whatever gross names you can come up with to match the theme—are nice in-school snacks, especially since the children probably won't eat dinner on Halloween anyway. If possible without making yourself look like a monster, encourage the children to save the candy for an after school treat.

Costumes and a parade are a must and tend to take up most of a traditional Halloween party. Makeup is fun but only practical if your school allows it, you have time for clean up, and you have *lots* of help as most children don't like waiting at Halloween—or any other time for that matter.

Traditional Party

This is probably the most traditional of all school parties. The treats and the costumes (tricking) are the party for the kids. Unfortunately, private, school, or community-sponsored parties are the only types that are safe anymore. Treats and dress-up will fill most of a party time but there are a few activities that can also be used for a more extended party.

ACTIVITIES

Quiet

Make spiders. See Little Miss Muffet section in chapter 10 or make the eating kind mentioned above.

Decorate your own cupcakes or sugar cookies. Provide plain cupcakes and plain cookies shaped like ghosts, pumpkins, cats, and/or witches. Let kids add icing and features of chocolate chips, raisins, candy corn, nuts, jelly beans, and the like.

Tell a ghost story or read one aloud.

Show a movie or filmstrip of the same.

Tell add-a-line ghost stories. Let children have their own ghost tales. You begin with a line like the old standby, "It was a dark and stormy night." Each child adds a sentence or a paragraph and leaves a cliffhanger for the next child to pick up, and the story builds around the circle.

Play a board game with a Halloween or ghost theme. *Clue* would certainly fit right in.

Shapes and straws. Use triangles for witches' hats, orange circles for jack-o'-lanterns.

Make place mats or other room and party decorations.

Stand-in-line

Pin-the-smile-on-the-jack-o'-lantern. Or Pin-the-Witch-on-the-Broom, or Pin-the-Black-Cat-on-the-Fence.

Bean Bag Toss. Toss a bean bag into a trick-or-treat bucket or sack, or toss a piece of candy and then let them eat it.

Active

Shoe race. Call it Witch's Relay and have children don a hat and ride a broom back to teammates.

Relay with a broom sweeping a ball or a can.

"Haunted" balloons. Use white or black balloons and let them play at keeping balloons in the air or trying to pop everyone else's balloon. To add a fun note, you might write ghostly riddles on the outside of the balloons and have slips of paper inside on which you have written the answers.

Witch, Witch, Ghost. This is Halloween's Duck, Duck, Goose.

Long-Term Project

The ideal way to turn a Halloween party into a long-term project is to let the children create a "haunted room": Children may spend several weeks organizing, planning, and creating a haunted house in their classroom or the gym and treat the rest of the building to tours through their mystical mansion. Younger elementary children might spend time at stations during the week or weeks before Halloween making their own costumes for trick-or-treating. In either case, a good field trip would be to visit a theatre and learn about costuming, set design, and/or makeup.

Alternate projects would be going to a play that focuses on creepy costuming, makeup, or set design; research topics about the beginnings and symbols of Halloween or just symbols in general; and famous ghost stories, myths, and legends.

There is an activity called "world in a Hershey bar," designed as a way to make children realize that their everyday lives are influenced by the entire world. Children study the various ingredients that go into making a chocolate bar, where they come from, where they are processed, where the wrapper is made, and so on. They learn that the chocolate comes from one place, is refined in another; sugar and nuts from somewhere else; the paper, printing, and retailing from still another; and that thousands of people from countries all over the world are involved in making the simple bar of chocolate they so enjoy begging for on Halloween night.

THANKSGIVING

Of course, for a Thanksgiving party, you must have a banquet, either "traditional American style" or "Pilgrims and Indians" style. See the historical and cultural chapters for additional ideas and activities. As it is with most feasts, eating and/or food preparation will be the focus of most of the activities at a Thanksgiving party. Traci's Cub Scouts went so far as to call their Thanksgiving party a *Pig-grims Day*. Each brought an appropriate treat to eat, and they spent most of the meeting eating.

Suffice it to say that there should be turkey in some form—turkey-shaped cookies, or turkeys made by kids with candy-corn tails stuck into icing of a plain round cookie, or just plain real turkey! In addition, any one or more of the usual accompaniments of Thanksgiving dinner are good—cranberry relish, cranberry jam and biscuits, corn on the cob, mashed potatoes, stuffing, corn bread, corn pudding, pumpkin anything (especially pie), any other kind of pies, sweet potato anything, and so on. You might want to compile a recipe book of the kids' favorite Thanksgiving dishes as made by their relatives. You could come dressed as a pilgrim, an Indian, or just the way you usually dress for Thanksgiving dinner.

Traditional Party

ACTIVITIES

Quiet

Read a book or story or watch a filmstrip about Thanksgiving or a related subject. Rip Van Winkle is good here.

Cook your own snack or make your own "meal."

Shapes and straws. Use ears of corn or turkey feathers for shapes.

Make Indian or pioneer vests from paper bags, or other woodland Indian crafts.

Stand-in-line

Pin-the-Feather-on-the-Turkey.

Bean Bag Toss. Toss the Turkey (bean bag) into the Barn (box decorated like a barn or just painted red).

Active

Chase the Turkey into the Barn. Use a broom or a stick to maneuver a ball into an opening in a box on the floor.

"Thanksgiving dinner." Class sits on chairs in a large circle. Number off so that each group has at least three people. Groups are named after parts of a Thanksgiving dinner: such as potatoes, gravy, turkey, cranberry sauce, and pumpkin pie. *It* stands in the middle, and **announces** that he or she would like something for Thanksgiving dinner and mentions one or more foods. "I think I'll have some potatoes and gravy and beans." Then children in those groups must change chairs. In the chaos, It also tries to take a chair. The child left standing is the new It.

Long-Term Project

Several class projects similar to ones used for other parties could be adapted for use here. As you measured out the size of a Conestoga wagon in Frontier Days, mark out the size of the passenger area of the Mayflower. Then try filling that area with the number of passengers that embarked on the Mayflower. Or taking a cue from the Dinosaur Days party, you might just measure and mark out the dimensions of the ship.

Children might work on such projects as writing and producing their own drama depicting the voyage of the Pilgrims, the landing on Plymouth Rock, or the first Thanksgiving; building models of the Mayflower, the Pilgrims' first homes, or the Indians' village; writing up a cookbook of the dishes that would have been served at the first Thanksgiving or a class cookbook of Thanksgiving family favorites; and/or illustrating the journey of the Pilgrims on maps with thumbtacks and yarn. Appropriate resource topics for this theme include religions of the Pilgrims, life of the Indians, conditions on the Mayflower, precolonial history, and tools and crafts of the Pilgrims.

WINTER WONDERLAND

In keeping with the current social trend of not observing religious holidays like Christmas and Easter, Hanukkah, and Passover in our public schools—even though we do celebrate other religiously based holidays like Halloween and St. Patrick's Day—we will stick to the generic winter theme. You may insert Christmas symbols such as Santa and his reindeer, elves, Christmas trees, wreaths, or a Hanukkah dreidel or menorah as you see fit.

Snacks suitable for a winter party include hot cocoa with marshmallows or candy-cane stirrers, egg nog, "pigs in blankets," snow cones, hot fudge sundaes, any traditional rolled cookies, any traditional ethnic delicacy like St. Lucia's wreath, fattimand, or pepparkakor.

Traditional/Extended Party

ACTIVITIES

Quiet

Read a story such as *The Big Snow* or *Frosty the Snow Man.*

Watch a filmstrip or video on a suitable theme.

Make gift wrap. Make a stamp with cut potato, carrot, citrus fruit or other veggies, and tempera or an ink pad. (Fruits and veggies of the same kind but not used for stamping could be snacks.)

Winter craft. Cut out snowflakes, make a picture of a snow scene with cotton balls, or finger paint with shaving cream on dark-colored paper.

Shapes and straws. Shapes could be snow men or their hats, snowballs, candy canes, and the like.

Stand-in-line

Pin-the-Hat-on-the-Snow-Man.

Dress a flannel-board doll or a regular doll for the weather.

Toss a "snowball" of crumpled paper at a hat.

Active

Outside:

Make a snow fort or a snow man in small groups.

Play Fox and Goose in the snow.

Make an obstacle course in the snow.

Inside:

Snow, Snow, Melt, or **Snow Man, Snow Man, Hat.** This is a Duck, Duck, Goose variation.

Parade. Act out being snow men. Be sure to slowly melt away!

Musical chairs. Play holiday songs and pretend to be reindeer looking for a place in the team.

Long-Term Project

A fun class project for a winter theme would be to make ice castles, which are a lot like sand castles—only colder. Have children fill a variety of wide-mouthed containers—jelly jars, plastic freezer dishes, soup cans—with water (a little added food color adds to the fun!) and freeze them outside overnight. The next day, thaw the containers inside for five minutes, then empty them outside. Use squirt bottles filled with warm water for glue, and let the kids create their own frozen fantasies. Helpful hint: Be sure to have plenty of spare mittens available.

Other appropriate activities for a winter project include making a crystal garden (use ammonia and bluing), making snow men and reindeer from long balloons (good for those of you in the sun belt who can't make real snow men), looking at snow under a microscope, and making a hail stone.

Related study topics might include snowflake patterns, which might lead you to other patterns in life and/or to quilts. Using fabric or paper, children might make a quilt block; they might even put all their blocks together to make a class quilt—as many pioneer women did in the winter months. Other research areas include crystals, seasons, planets, winter traditions around the world, the North or South Pole and explorations, penguins, seals, reindeer, tundra, and how candy is made.

GROUNDHOG DAY

To celebrate Groundhog Day, you might act out the story, check the weather, visit a weather station, make shadow monsters (trace around shadow on paper taped to a wall, then add features), and make groundhog stick puppets including a black one for the shadow. Snacks for such a party could include a variety of veggies, a little bark (chocolate cookies), and a cool drink after all that exposure to the hot sun!

MY FUNNY VALENTINE

Traditional Party

Valentine's Day, a customary party day at school, has "traditions" that are hard to change, so enjoy them; the kids certainly do. In fact, Valentine's Day is usually one of the children's favorite celebrations. Why? We think the reason is twofold. First, the entire day is devoted to telling others you like them and hearing from others how much they like you; it's a day of being nice to each other, universally. Naturally this shower of mutual affection makes kids feel good about themselves and their classmates. Don't touch that tradition—it's a keeper! The second reason is that it is the party over which they have the most control. They make the valentines, they make the decorations, they make the mailboxes, they do the exchange and, except in kindergarten and first grade, they read the cards. The major activity at a Valentine's Day party is reading cards—and who created that activity? The kids. It is in every sense *their* party. Child involvement is what we like to see so don't try to change a good thing.

Cupcakes and cookies are the traditional snacks at Valentine's Day—usually heart-shaped cookies iced in pink or red or cupcakes with like frosting. Why not be different? How about ice cream sundaes? Scoop the ice cream into colorful plastic cups before heading for school. This saves time and allows you to go through the day somewhat unsticky. Muffin tins make good trays, and with squeeze bottles of syrups and sprinkles or cherries a do-it-yourself line is ready for action. For a less sugary treat, serve finger sandwiches cut into heart shapes, filling them with pink or red foods like ham salad, bologna, or strawberried cream cheese. Veggies and dips go over well if you serve them on heart-shaped doilies on a fancy tray with dip in a fancy bowl. (When she served as Valentine's Day hostess, Traci used her etched chrome tray and cut glass bowl; the second-graders appreciated being treated like grownups at a fancy tea.)

Wear red or pink or white, or dress formally. A heart can be painted on your or the children's cheeks with clown makeup by just overlapping two finger prints. Red-checkered table cloths add to the festivity.

As we mentioned, the activities for the traditional party are pretty much predetermined and need to be left alone. The following, therefore, apply better to an extended party or the culmination party of a long-term project. If you'd like to choose one activity to add to a traditional party, feel free.

ACTIVITIES

Quiet

Make snack. Let kids put together finger sandwiches or decorate their own cookies or cupcakes.

Make goody bags or place mats if not done beforehand.

Read story, or watch a filmstrip or video.

Shapes and straws. How about hearts for the shapes?

Play a game of the card game Hearts.

Stand-in-line

Pin-the-Heart-in-the-Valentine-Mailbox. Or Pin-Arrows-on-Cupid's Bow.

Bean Bag Toss. Toss a red beanbag into a lacy basket.

Have a smile contest with awards (applause or make your own valentines) for loudest giggle, deepest dimples, widest smile, most braces, and so forth.

Have a laugh face-off. Divide group into two facing rows, taking turns and no touching allowed. Have one group and then the other try to make their opponents laugh or smile. Children sit down when "out."

Active

Heart, Heart, Valentine. This is a Duck, Duck, Goose variation.

Circle game. For younger children, stand in a circle and sing "Will You Be My Valentine?" to the tune of "London Bridge is Falling Down," while passing a large red heart. The person holding the heart at the end of the song is "out."

Dance. Play or sing the above tune and skip in a circle.

See chapter 10 on *Through the Looking Glass* for more related ideas on hearts.

Long-Term Project

A good way to turn Valentine's Day into a long-term study for older children is for the class to study the history of Valentine's Day, a holiday observed as far back as the early Roman Empire with many legends and national traditions. Every year an article about the history of Valentine's Day appears in at least one magazine or newspaper. Watch for such pieces; use them to read aloud to younger kids, as research sources for older ones, and/or as bulletin board material. Children might also like studying the history of the greeting card, particularly the Valentine's Day card. Someone in your area who collects old valentines might come and share his or her knowledge and collection with the children. Other related avenues of study would include Cupid, lace, tatting, pinpricking, riddles, famous love stories, the St. Valentine's Day massacre, and others. Don't forget such projects as making and sending Valentines to shut-ins, the elderly in nursing homes, the pediatrics ward at your hospital, servicemen and women, or pen pals.

HAIL TO THE CHIEF

In the month of February, we as a nation observe the birthdays of George Washington and Abraham Lincoln. Martin Luther King's birthday is observed in late January. You may prefer to host a party celebrating one of these men or you might combine all three into a leadership theme or a patriotic theme. Simply adjust the snacks and activities appropriately.

Snacks for a party including the celebration of George Washington's birthday should, of course, center around cherries. If you wish to include Abe Lincoln, ants on a log (celery with cream cheese or peanut butter and raisins) are a natural treat. For Martin Luther King, you might want to include examples of southern cooking.

To add an authentic flavor to your party, you could wear a period outfit or simply dress all in red, white, and blue. Paper products and tableware could carry out this color scheme or feature stickers of any of these men.

Traditional/Extended Party

ACTIVITIES

Quiet

Make red, white, and blue place mats.

Lotto. Use a page with all the presidents.

Do a guessing game about the presidents. For example, "I know a president who was born in Ohio, was quite overweight, and whose name began with T."

Word games. Try using the names of the presidents in a sentence. "I've been washing a ton of laundry," for example. Kids like bad puns. Or see how many words you can make from the letters in the name of the featured man.

Read a story about a president, or watch a filmstrip or video.

Make a tricornered hat. Cut three semicircles and connect them with staples at the corners.

Write a group story about what children would do as president.

Stand-in-line

Pin-the-Cherry-in-the-Tree. Or Pin-the-Hat-on-Lincoln or Pin-the-Tie-on-King.

Bean Bag Toss. Toss a bean bag into a log—a potato chip can covered with brown paper.

Toss a coin across the Delaware. Have a contest to see how far children can toss a coin.

Active

George, George, Abe, or **Martin, Martin, King.** This is a variation on Duck, Duck, Goose.

Musical chairs. Call this variation Washington Crossing the Delaware. Make two marks on the floor several feet apart and several feet long. This is the Delaware River. The little Washingtons are to cross back and forth across the river until the music stops. If they are in the middle of the river when the music stops they fell out of the boat and are out of the game for that round.

Lincoln's up. This can be a race between two or three children or just fun practice of a motor skill. Put four pennies in front of each person on the table. At the signal, the children are to flip their pennies with a pancake turner so that Lincoln is up.

Play tiddlywinks with pennies.

Parade. Include lots of drums (as always, check this one out with the school!)

Long-Term Project

In keeping with this theme, children could do research on a president or presidents. Each child could present the finished project to the class and display it. On celebration day, children could dress in the period of their president and come to an inaugural ball and banquet. Alternatively, the class could participate in a class mock election, with students taking parts of past, current, or pretend candidates for national office or as candidates for class office: campaigning and debating, designing posters, writing slogans and speeches, or memorizing real speeches of famous candidates. The finale for such a project would, of course, be election day.

YOUNGER THAN SPRINGTIME

Arbor Day is a perfect focus for a worthwhile school party and one holiday that seems to have been overlooked in the past few decades. Do you remember leaving your elementary classroom on an early spring afternoon and planting a tree on the school grounds or at a park nearby or collecting pennies to buy trees for the downtown square? Arbor Day observations are more a part of our memories or even our parents' memories than our children's. And yet what is more fitting in these times of environmental crisis than to focus attention on our natural surroundings and our responsibilities in maintaining them?

For snacks at such a party, serve anything that comes from a tree—apples, pears, cherries, peaches, and nuts. Cookies shaped as trees or animals that live in trees—birds, eggs, squirrels—would be appropriate. Drink apple cider, and use lots of green in your decorations and paper products.

Traditional/Extended Party

ACTIVITIES

Quiet

Make a forest in a bottle. Use a small, clear container like a 35mm film canister. Put in a layer of dirt, a layer of grass or moss, wood chips, a piece of leaf or pine needle, and an eyedropperful of water. (These represent respectively, soil so the tree could grow, what is around the tree, the tree, and water for continued survival.) A yellow smile sticker on the top stands for the sunshine. Put a tree sticker on the side of the tube.

Sing a song about trees.

Read "Trees" by Joyce Kilmer.

As a class or in small groups, **make a list** of all the things that trees are good for.

Stand-in-line

Pin-the-Leaf-on-the-Tree. Or Pin-the-Egg-on-the-Nest-in-the-Tree.

Bean Bag Toss. Plant the seed (bean bag) in the ground (potato chip can covered in brown paper).

Active

Play "Here We Go Round the Mulberry Bush."

Tree, Tree, Branch, or **Elm, Elm, Oak** for Duck, Duck, Goose, or Drop the Handkerchief using an acorn or walnut instead of a handkerchief.

Plant a tree.

Long-Term Project

For larger projects, identify some trees. There are some fun games that help children with this. A big chart of tree identification or the anatomy of a tree would be good for bulletin boards. Study your local parks and neighborhoods and determine where there is a need for tree planting. Sponsor a class project in raising funds and purchasing trees for needy areas. Study how trees help the environment. Send for information from the Treepeople or the National Arbor Day Foundation organizations dedicated to planting trees. Contact your area conservation clubs, agricultural referral agencies, and state forestry departments. Investigate the lives of trees, the impact trees have on the ecology, the plant and animal life around them, and the human life around them—physically and psychologically. Consider the number of products that come from trees. Take field trips to nearby forests, nature centers, and parks; observe the impact trees have on the area; and go on nature hikes.

SUMMARY

There's a full year of holiday parties, but there are still many other holidays left for your imaginations to transform into fun, meaningful, unique school parties with a purpose. Let your children's imaginations be your guide and have a nice party!

RESOURCES

Childcraft: The How and Why Library. Vols. 3, 6, 9, 11. Chicago, Ill.: World Book, Childcraft International, Inc., 1980.

Chupick, Carol Orava. *Celebrate Autumn.* Carthage, Ill.: Shining Star Publications, 1985.

Harelson, Randy. *The Kids' Diary of 365 Amazing Days.* New York: Workman Publishing, 1979.

Hartwig, Judy. *Celebrate Winter.* Carthage, Ill.: Shining Star Publications, 1985.

Holzbauer, Beth. *Creative Crafts for Young Children.* Chicago, Ill.: Children's Press, 1986.

Mackenthum, Carol. *Celebrate Summer.* Carthage, Ill.: Shining Star Publications, 1985.

Marks, Burton, and Marks, Rita. *The Spook Book.* New York: Lothrop, Lee and Shepard, 1981.

National Arbor Day Foundation. 100 Arbor Ave., Nebraska City, Neb. 68419.

Supraner, Robyn. *Happy Halloween: Things to Make and Do.* Mahwah, N.J.: Troll Associates, 1981.

Treepeople. 12601 Mulholland Dr., Beverly Hills, Calif. 90210.

Part 3
The Party's Over But....

12 But What Else Can I Do?

Classroom Volunteer Opportunities

Most familiar and most appealing to parents is the volunteer work that enables them to be with their children in the classroom. The kinds of activities that parents can get involved with may depend a good deal on the teacher's classroom style, the needs of the class, and how comfortable the teacher is with their presence. Working within these parameters, though, parents can provide many ongoing services. There are also some interesting short-term ideas they can share with the teacher and students that allow them to do what interests them.

This chapter lists examples of ways parents can contribute for perhaps an hour or two a week over the school year. None of these requires any particular expertise or special training, but each offers the children a positive experience and fills gaps left by our system of one teacher trying to meet the needs of twenty-five or more children at once.

ONE-ON-ONE ACTIVITIES

Listen to children read aloud. This may be the only opportunity children get to practice. If you wish, it is quite easy to tie an award-reward program in with this activity. Simply give out prizes for books read aloud: a sticker after five, a smelly sticker after ten, a bookmark after twenty-five, and so on. This volunteer activity also gives you the unique opportunity of memorizing volumes of popular children's literature. Would you like us to recite *In a Dark, Dark Room* or *Mr. Brown Can Moo,* two early-reader favorites we've heard at least seventeen hundred times?

Assist with flash card drills. It's a dirty job, but somebody's got to do it. Memorization cannot be denied, so be a flasher in math, vocabulary, spelling, alphabet, colors, numbers, number words, color words, shape recognition, and others.

Provide individual help. This kind of activity can include anything from assisting with work sheets to helping with beginning writing. (Traci fondly recalls the time she was floating around a room of busy writers answering questions about spelling, capitals, sentencing, etc. One youngster asked, "How do you spell *wants*?" "W-a-n-t-s," Traci replied without looking at his paper. Later she walked by his desk and glanced at his work. His story began, "Wants upon a time....")

Practice vocabulary with non-English-speaking students.

Work with underachievers. This kind of tutoring may require just that you sit down with a child in a secluded area of the room or quiet corner of the hall and provide individual attention as the child works through regular classroom assignments, or you may be offering specialized instruction from separate texts or work sheets.

Assist individuals with makeup work.

Help children learn to type or keyboard on computer.

Help write or run programs on the computer.

Work with a handicapped child. This type of volunteering includes activities as simple as providing physical assistance to and from various points in the building to scribing (writing as child dictates) to reading aloud to the visually impaired to helping with simple motor skills. As more and more physically handicapped children are mainstreamed into the regular classroom, more volunteer support will be needed.

Help children select library books. Young children may need supervision and guidance during visits to the school library.

Escort children to bathroom, office, library, or cafeteria.

Help with handwriting practice.

Drill spelling words.

Help young children with walking on a balance beam, jumping rope, or skipping. Kindergartners especially need to be tested in the areas of gross motor skills; you can be a big help.

Help students who play instruments. Musical instruction is an enrichment area in which volunteers can offer support and programming. Even if you have little musical talent, you can listen to children practice an instrument in the same way one listens to beginning readers practice reading aloud.

SMALL-GROUP ACTIVITIES

Play and teach instructional and/or popular board games. This activity includes playing any of the games designed specifically for increasing students' skills in math, geography, and science, for example, or just playing such games as Candyland, Parcheesi, chess, and cards. (See chapter 3.)

Tell stories to children. Storytelling is a fine art and one which is becoming extinct in the face of television and movies. Keeping the tradition alive enables children to explore the images of their own imaginations.

Play games at recess. Teachers, particularly at small schools, may appreciate relief from playground duty. Surely almost any of us could spend a half-hour leading rounds of Red Rover or Dodge Ball.

Make sets for plays. Anne MacLeod, volunteer parent in Newport News, Virginia, tells of the scenic backdrop she and several other parents made for her daughter Elizabeth's second grade. Their work was so good, the backdrop was kept and used again and again. Several years later, the teacher invited the parents and their children back to see "their" set being used as her fifth-grade class presented the same play. "Elizabeth and I and our friends had many pleasant memories," Ms. MacLeod writes. "It made for much good fun."

Make puppets, costumes, props for plays.

Play a musical instrument. If you have a musical talent, share it. You may not only entertain the little ones, you may just inspire a future maestro—or at least interest some in taking lessons.

Help children learn a foreign language. Experts agree that foreign languages should be learned young—in elementary school. Yet our school systems, for whatever reasons, simply do not or cannot begin teaching languages until middle school, junior high, or even high school. Can you speak Spanish, French, German, Russian, Japanese? You don't have to be fluent; even rudimentary knowledge can be beneficial to children.

Help with cooking projects.

Set up experiments. You don't have to be the scientific expert. The teacher can tell what she needs or buy a book by Mr. Wizard. All you have to do is get together the materials and set up the show.

Set up a "grocery store" to practice math skills. Great fun for primary grades. Bring empty containers with prices on them, a play cash register and/or a couple of calculators, and play money, and you've set up a wonderful learning exercise.

Show a filmstrip to the group.

Supervise a craft.

Supervise groups taking tests.

Take attendance.

Collect lunch money.

Collect permission slips.

Check out audiovisual equipment.

In addition to these rather generic activities, you may have special skills you are willing to share with the students in your child's classroom. Perhaps you could teach a craft at which you are skilled. Do you have a hobby or collection that you can share? Use your culinary skills to teach some special recipes. Do you have specialized career skills you'd like to share? Use your particular expertise in your child's classroom.

E.C. (EXTRACLASSROOM) SERVICES

Parents can help in many ways without actually being in the classroom. Attention working parents: These may be for you!

Help contact parents through telephone trees or class newsletters.

Assist with field trips.

Gather resource materials.

Check out books from the public library.

Make a list of library resources.

Visit a sick child at home.

Read stories aloud into a tape recorder.

Make instructional games.

Make reading carrels from boxes.

PAPER PUSHING AND PAPER CUTTING

Lastly, there are any number of clerical, organizational, or generally helpful activities that you can do to relieve your classroom teacher. Some of these can be done at home; some may need to be done at school. Some require familiarity with office machines; some require tidiness and precision; some are merely brainless, stress-free jobs that somebody has to do, so why not veg out and help out all at once!

Reproduce materials.

Collate and staple.

Grade papers.

Record grades.

Prepare bulletin boards.

Prepare teaching materials such as cutouts for calendars, cutouts for crafts, counted items for math skills, etc.

Laminate materials.

Color posters.

Take class inventory and/or replenish supplies.

KINDERGARTEN SKILLS

Several years ago, in Waupun, Wisconsin, teachers were awarded a federal grant to devise a series of developmentally sequenced skills for young children. The program was intended to prepare children for reading. Prereading skills were identified and divided into the general categories of motor, visual, auditory, and verbal. Activities were designed to focus on and develop each of these generalized skills. The format was such that small groups of children could be moved through levels of skills using a sort of station system so that children of varying readiness levels could be taught in one classroom simultaneously.

Kindergarten teachers in Cedar Rapids, Iowa, found this format very beneficial. Dividing the children into small groups and allowing them to work on these skills on a daily basis provided the kind of immediate guidance, feedback, and praise that one teacher simply cannot give every member of class every day.

Here is a program ripe with volunteer opportunities. Every day it requires the support of several adults—one for each group of five to six children. In Cedar Rapids, the groups are led by the teacher, two teacher's aides, and two volunteers. Staffing and scheduling the program is a major undertaking, but one well worth the time. (The program is, in fact, the reason for a paid volunteer coordinator; the program was set up as a magnet program to desegregate a school overpopulated—according to state and federal standards—by minority students. Since so many volunteers were required to staff the skills program, desegregation funds paid to employ a volunteer coordinator.)

Volunteers agree to come to school one half-day a week or every other week. Each meets in half-hour sessions with groups of children from each of the kindergartens. For each session, kindergarten teachers have prepared a packet including instructions for the leader of the group and materials and/or work sheets for carrying out the instructions for that day's skills. Activities are simple and straightforward so that even novice skills leaders can read their instructions and lead the group without previous preparation. Instructions lead the skills helper through the session step by step, including a brief explanation of the point of the activity, opening instructional remarks, directions for carrying out the activity, suitable remarks of encouragement, possible obstacles to children's success, and a related activity to fill in any extra time for fast groups.

Kindergarten skills has proven a very successful program in readying children for first-grade reading skills, but skills helpers do a lot more for the school and the children than just teach reading skills. They also teach group cooperation, school pride, positive self-concepts, and community spirit. And the skills program provides the volunteer program with a healthy start; parents begin as skills helpers and continue as volunteers for years.

OTHER CONTRIBUTIONS

The possibilities for classroom volunteering are endless. At least, it seems so if we take a page from the brainstorming session of a group of parents interested in setting up minilabs in their children's classrooms. Minilabs, as these parents conceived them, are short-term instructional sessions conducted by parents or other resource people for small groups of children either in the classroom or at suitable sites outside the building—a parent's kitchen, the science museum, a city park. The following topics for minilabs were thought up in one 1989 session by a group of parents and children.

Parents' Ideas	Students' Ideas
video lab	party-food making
hot air ballooning	stuffed animals
airport—cockpit, control tower	TLC baby-sitting methods
nature center	environmental study
plant identification	horseback riding
Czech Village museum	home construction
hospital visit	Bird Brain
orienteering—maps, compass	pet shop
courtroom, jail, mock trial	fire station
radio station	animal care
dairy farm	knit, crochet, cross-stitch
economics—bank, vault	zoo tour
frog dissection	business visit
Amana Colonies	high school tour
manufacturing plant	gov't buildings visit
theatre	radio, TV stations visit
train ride	batteries and bulbs
Pioneer Village	board games
ceramic studio	art, drawing
raptors	musical instruments
police station	health career visits
fire station	free work time
nuclear power station	ping-pong contest
medical lab	barber/beautician visit

art museum
Seminole Valley Farm (historical)
artist's study
outdoor activities
ice cream plant tour
middle school tour
fabric art
papermaking
horseback riding
aviation
origami
creative dramatics
child care
service projects
student band
stuffed animals
music exploration
American Sign Language
book covers
nature center—snakes
dentist office
fitness lab
art show
adopt a grandparent
career day
physics
school improvement projects
magician/magic tricks

Nintendo
visit large engineering/industrial plant
birds, nature
Star Trek film fest
Star Wars film fest
chemistry
cooking—pizza, cookies
gym recreation
war vehicles
preschool visit
sewing
first aid
science experiments
puppets
body
rubbings
models
dancing trip
library
sky walk tour
historical homes
lawyer's office
police station
bakery
university science labs
baseball field—pro players
veterinarian
bowling
ducks
amusement park
science station
airport
dentist's office
back of grocery store
post office

Obviously there are many, many possibilities for classroom opportunities; you are limited only by your outlook and your time. So what if you know nothing about raptors—or even what they are. Pick up the phone. You can find experts to help in almost any field and you can see that children are willing and interested in a wide variety of learning avenues—including such "intellectual" pursuits as Nintendo and amusement parks! Oh well, did we say they had to stop being kids?

13 The Little Idea That Grew—A Success Story Written by Volunteers

Ongoing All-School Programs

Once upon a time in the land of Iowa, a wise and good principal looked about his kingdom of Johnson Elementary School and saw a need. "My children," Stephen, the Wise and the Good said to himself, "need to feel good about their writing. We need to show them that at our school, writing is important."

The good principal called upon one of his loyal volunteers to help him, and together Steve Chambliss and Laura Derr established a writing recognition program which they dubbed Writers Workshop.

The program was simple in design. Each month every classroom teacher chose one or two young writers for participation. A week before the workshop, Laura and Julie Sawyers, a friend roped into helping, photographed and interviewed each writer, asking questions like, "When's your birthday?" "What do you want to be when you grow up?" and "What is your favorite book?" Also about a week before the workshop, the students' original manuscripts were submitted to the office. There a loyal secretary typed them and sent them to the school board production office where they were printed up into a booklet.

On the day of the workshop, Laura brought a lavish feast—cookies and juice—and participants were invited to a "party" to share treats and their stories. Since there were up to twenty participants a month, the writers were separated into two groups of eight to ten. During the workshop, participants took turns reading their stories aloud to their group. After one finished reading, he or she asked the group, "What do you like about my story?" The author called upon the others to comment positively on the story. Laura was the leader in the sense that she guided the students toward making specific comments, but she raised her hand to speak and generally participated like another student. Only positive comments were solicited in Writers Workshop and no criticism of any kind was allowed.

Grade levels were mixed at all workshops, which worked very well. It was a lovely experience to watch and listen to fifth- and sixth graders find sincere appreciation for first-grade efforts and to observe little ones unable to read for themselves listen intently to the older ones' stories and make telling and profound remarks about them.

In addition to a copy of that month's booklet, each participant was given a school pencil and a plastic button sporting the Writers Workshop logo—made with a PTA button machine—and festooned with a ribbon bearing the student's name. After the workshop, the original copies of the student writings, the photos, and interview information were displayed on the bulletin board in the main hallway of the school. There every student, every staff member, and every visitor to the building was sure to spot them. At the end of the month the stories and pictures were given back to the students.

In just a couple of months, the success of the program was apparent. Being chosen to participate in Writers Workshop was an honor that every student longed to attain. Writing became almost instantly a valued activity in the eyes of every child and every teacher. Such a visible display was great P.R. for the building. Parents liked seeing the student writing prominently displayed on the bulletin board; they began asking about the program. Parents of participants shared the booklet with friends and family. Soon everyone was interested in and took pride in the writing program. After a time, since the "Workshop" title was really a misnomer in that no suggestions for changes were ever made to the writing, the name of the program was changed to Writers Showcase.

The wise and good principal was pleased. His loyal volunteer was proud. All the people in the kingdom were happy, and it was good.

This is not a fairy tale at all, but a true story, and one that is easy to emulate. For the first several years of its existence, Writers Showcase was coordinated by just two volunteers with the help and support of the teaching staff and the school secretary. Then two new volunteers stepped in to run the workshop on alternate months while another volunteer photographed and did the bulletin board. One year, the coordinators did the typing. The next year, the school did the typing again, but the program went back to just one volunteer taking care of everything. Over the eight years of its existence, Showcase has been coordinated by four different people and assisted by five or six others, but despite volunteer turnover the program remains as popular with the children and as effective as ever.

The beauty of this program is that it can be handled by just a few volunteers working perhaps five hours a month at minimal cost. Coordinating a program such as this is not a taxing burden on a volunteer, and it is one that can be easily transferred from one volunteer to another. Training is minimal; all a volunteer really needs to run it are good listening skills and a caring heart. Good writing skills are a plus, but not necessary.

It's still not happily-ever-after time, though; the name of this fable is "The Little Idea that *Grew.*" Writers Showcase is the little idea, and it grew into many other things. The first offshoot the showcase sprouted was called Writers Express. Laura Derr, our original Showcase volunteer, soon encountered one young writer who was not satisfied with just the recognition of the school. She wanted *more.* She wanted to be *published*!

Laura began working with this student to help her polish and perfect her writing, edit the grammar and punctuation, and prepare a clean, final copy to be submitted for publication. Laura typed final copies, went to the library and researched periodicals that published children's writings — she was then unaware of the rich resources of local and regional publications using student work — and sent them off for possible publication. Eventually Laura and her aspiring author were successful; the young writer saw her name in print in a national magazine.

The news spread, and more children clamored for the opportunity of submitting their writing for publication outside the building. Before long Laura was overwhelmed by eager writers. Like any wise volunteer she turned to her friends and neighbors and friends of neighbors and coerced them into helping. In a matter of months, this new program had a name, Writers Express, and a core of eight to ten volunteers meeting with children in many classrooms. From one volunteer offering help to one student, the program grew into many volunteers offering an hour or more a week to listen to scores of children's stories. Individual volunteers then went home and typed stories which they sent to Laura. Laura sorted through all the children's manuscripts, choosing those most likely to succeed, mailing off submissions, and filling out certificates for every participant in the program.

Before long the program no longer dealt with talented writers justifiably interested in possible publication, but with lots of warm young bodies and fertile minds whose manuscripts, though probably unsuitable for publication, were nonetheless worthy of someone's attention. Quickly, the emphasis of Writers Express shifted from publication to conferencing. The point of participating in Writers Express was no longer just to get a piece of writing ready for publication, but also to provide a time in which every writer was allowed to share the writing with a caring listener, to get lots of positive feedback, and to begin examining the possibility of revising the writing. More volunteers were recruited and trained in improving their listening skills, perfecting positive responses, and forming questions that led young writers to reach a little beyond themselves—all skills necessary for leading writing conferences.

In five years, Writers Express grew from one volunteer working with one outstanding writer to twenty-five volunteers conferencing with upwards of five hundred writers a year and submitting well over two hundred pieces of writing for publication or display in various forums outside the school building. Writers Express certainly was a little idea that grew!

Still our tale is not over. No sooner did the Writers Express program begin to hit its stride than one of the volunteers came up with the bright idea that kindergartners and pre-first-graders could profit from a similar program to help them get started writing. As any parent of a very young child knows, four- and five-year-olds are more than ready to tell any number of stories; the only obstacle to their being writers is that they can't write. So why should scribing get in the child's way; an adult could get down on paper what little ones dictate, couldn't they? Thus was born another writing program at Johnson Elementary, this one titled Springboard. Suddenly, there came to be in the kingdom twelve good women who donated an hour per week to sit down with young children and a box of crayons and a blank piece of paper and create an original, illustrated story.

Needless to say, the volunteer writing program soon became unwieldy and burdensome. By now our good and wise volunteer Laura Derr had bowed out entirely and had passed the baton on to now two volunteer coordinators. They in turn delegated coordination of Springboard to another volunteer. The school found funds to hire a typist to deal with the scores of submissions being produced every month. Still, finding enough volunteers to service every classroom became a major headache. Just as soon as there were enough volunteers trained and plugged in, one would get a job, another would have a baby, another's spouse was transferred. There were never enough adults, and by now teachers were so supportive of the program they not only expected a volunteer, they practically demanded one.

Necessity certainly was the mother of the invention in the case of the Junior Volunteer program. No, there weren't enough adults out there available to volunteer, but there were, right in the building, fifth-graders who by now had been conferencing in Writers Express for three years. They certainly were as qualified as most adults to lead a conference with first- and second-graders. Thanks to a new, very wise and open principal, Cynthia Monroe, and her agreeable staff, this latest idea grew wings. After several training sessions, thirteen eager fifth-graders began leading writing conferences with awed but willing first- and second-graders.

Junior Volunteers is now in its third year, and a lot more than writing is being learned in those conferences. Fifth-graders are learning responsibility, sharing, and respect while finely tuning their own writing skills. They are learning how to deal gently and kindly with younger students of all personalities, and they are learning that adults trust them to do so. The little ones are learning to trust their older peers, to open up their minds to a caring listener, as well as how to feel comfortable as a writer. They are learning that their school is a place where people care about each other and help each other and where the fifth-graders don't ignore or tease the little ones on the playground anymore; instead they wave and call them by name and ask them if they've written any good stories lately.

By now in the kingdom of Johnson School, certainly writing is a valued activity. Interest in writing is evident everywhere. This is apparent as you enter the foyer and immediately come upon the newest facet of the writing program, the Writers Cupboard.

For a whole year, a big, old, ugly, brown cupboard graced the back hallway of Johnson School. Empty and awkward, it served no purpose where it stood, and there was really no place to put the darned thing. But one day, our good and open-minded principal looked upon the cupboard and saw not an ugly object in her way, but a possibility. "Why not," whispered Mrs. Monroe to her writing program coordinators, "transform this ugly old thing into a Writers Cupboard?" And so it was done.

One talented volunteer was recruited to stencil pink hearts and blue flowers on the front of the cupboard as well as the words *Writers Cupboard*. Suddenly the old cupboard wasn't ugly and drab, but cheerful and bright. It was moved to the front hallway, and with the help of volunteers and staff was filled with all sorts of paper and fancy pencils. On one of its shelves were a couple of dictionaries and a thesaurus. An old typewriter found its place on a table next to the cupboard, and the area was filled with child-sized tables and chairs for writers.

For the grand opening, the cupboard was decorated with hats of all shapes and kinds as inspiration for story writing. On the first day the cupboard was open, each class was invited to an orientation. Children were introduced to the purpose of the cupboard — to be a resource for writing materials and a quiet place writers could come to work or to confer — and shown all the goodies inside the cupboard for their enjoyment. There were only three rules for the writing cupboard area: (1) Be quiet; (2) all materials — except paper on which you have written — should be left in the cupboard; and (3) have fun!"

During the year, one volunteer refilled supplies and changed the theme of decorations for the cupboard area every month or so. Halloween was a big hit, with lots of appropriate decorations, a contest to name a plastic jack-o-lantern, and add-a-line story that began, "It was a dark and stormy Halloween night." Since then, the area has been decorated for major, nonreligious holidays, or filled with inspirational material to suit a theme. For example, February was poetry month: Any number of poems were displayed, poetry books and a rhyming dictionary were available, and one day a guest poet held a poet's corner.

While one volunteer has been responsible for upkeep of the area in its first year and a half, next year this responsibility will be turned over to the children. Classrooms will sign up for a month during which they will be in charge of decorations, inspirations displays, and keeping supplies available. This will give even more ownership to the kids and generate that much more interest in writing. It also should provide a valuable volunteer lesson, one that has been learned and practiced particularly well by the Junior Leagues: Volunteers can be valuable in creating, planning, and setting up a program and can serve the school and the program equally well by then stepping out of the program and handing over control to appropriate members of the school family.

Thus, the good and wise principals and the loyal volunteers looked upon their work and were glad. Their accomplishments were mighty and the children of their domain were happy and proud as they enthusiastically expressed themselves through writing. And so they lived happily ever after ... or at least until the next volunteer comes up with another great idea!

So it can be for you and the loyal subjects at your school. All of this merely demonstrates what can be accomplished when a supportive administration combines with a willing and creative volunteer network.

The lessons to be learned from our parable of Johnson School are these.

1. *Administrators, staff, and volunteers need to work together to coordinate effective all-school programs.* In our example, the principal called upon volunteers who relied on teachers and secretarial staff to support the program.

2. *Programs should be established to meet a clear and apparent need.* In our instance, the principal recognized that need — the need to put a higher value on writing. That also happened to coincide with a district goal to put more emphasis on writing. To determine needs, ask the administration, and the

teachers what kind of enrichment would they value. Research district proposals; read the district publications listing long-term goals. In Melinda's opinion, volunteer-supported writing programs seem to be ideal outlets for such programs because writing is one skill that can be effectively taught merely through encouragement. Make children feel good about their writing and they will want to write. The more they write, the better they get at it. Writing is therefore an area in which volunteers can contribute substantially to the learning process just by being good listeners and enthusiastic cheerleaders.

3. *Start simple and small.* Our now multifaceted writing program began with one simple idea, a party to celebrate writing. Volunteers and administrators worked together to establish a clear, consistent, easily managed methodology. Note, too, that teacher authority in the classroom or in the teaching process was not threatened in any way by this program. Teachers chose participants and allowed them to leave the classroom at a specified time. The actual sharing session did not teach writing skills, but simply praised work already done. Costs and time commitments were minimal. The PTA paid for film and processing and for school pencils and Showcase buttons for a total investment of about ten dollars a month. The school budget absorbed the costs of the publications—amazingly only about five dollars an issue! Volunteers donated goodies for the party which amounted to about five dollars—with really good cookies and real juice. Managing the entire program required about five work-hours a month from volunteers and required no particular expertise except self-confidence and a good rapport with children.

4. *Delegate.* Our heroine in this tale, Laura Derr, will be the first to tell you not to take all the responsibility on your shoulders. Grab a friend, a cohort in crime; support each other even at the earliest, simplest stages. Lean on everybody you can find; it's more fun and it's less frightening than hanging out there on your own.

5. *Be flexible, be creative, and be open to new ideas.* None of the programs we have discussed would have come into being if the volunteers and staff involved had not been open to suggestions. Except for Writers Showcase, each of these programs evolved slowly and out of a necessity that wasn't even there until someone used a new awareness and recognized a need. There is no room in creative volunteering for the "that's-the-way-we've-always-done-it" mentality.

Certainly the writing program at Johnson School is not unique; there exist many such examples of ongoing, all-school volunteer projects involving writing. Volunteer Pamela Hunter tells us of the Writing Center in her school, Grace Abbot Elementary School in Omaha, Nebraska, where volunteers assist children in creating their own illustrated books. A similar program keeps volunteers in Bettendorf, Iowa, involved with student writing. A teacher at Madison Elementary School in Cedar Rapids organized an after-school writing club. It is easy to see that the writing tutor concept is very fertile ground for creative volunteering in our schools.

Of course, there are many other on-going, all-school volunteer programs. Another popular concept is the Art-in-a-Suitcase or Picture Person program. Volunteers with some expertise in fine arts, select a collection of prints by famous artists and prepare a presentation for each print. They visit the classrooms sharing and discussing a different piece of art each month. This valuable enrichment program is easily established and carried out as long as there are artistic-minded volunteers in your area. Should your school fail to find an appropriate volunteer, check with your local art museum or art society for help. In fact, your PTA can purchase an entire Picture Person program. To send for more information see the resource list at the end of this chapter.

Also available for purchase is the Junior Great Books Program, a reading and discussion study program designed for children in third through twelfth grades. Volunteers must attend two full days of training, guidelines for which are dictated by the Great Books Foundation. This is an excellent enrichment program, and one that can be implemented after the training without an unreasonable time commitment. However, it does require that volunteers have some innate interest in and love of literature. For more information write to the Great Books Foundation, listed at the end of this chapter.

High school students in Connecticut began a creative program that would be great for elementary school volunteers to imitate. At Enfied High School students put together what they called Lab Carts, essentially portable resources centers. After constructing a simple set of shelves and mounting them on wheels, students gathered many multimedia materials all dealing with one area of interest; say, Africa or American Indians. They also put together an introductory sound-slide presentation that stimulated interest in the topic and instructed students how to use the materials included. The carts held books, records, tapes, bibliographies, other sound-slide programs, and lists of outside resources such as germane places to visit in and around the city and appropriate local guest speakers.

Other all-school programs demanding support from volunteers include the production of a school newsletter, a parent hospitality committee that greets new families and takes responsibility for staff appreciation and safety committees responsible for designating "safe houses" or "block homes" around the school district and setting up an adult crossing-guard network. Many schools are establishing programs involving senior citizens interacting with youngsters in a variety of roles. Contact local social workers working in the geriatric community and discuss ways you can initiate programs involving older citizens. Computer tutoring is another good area for volunteer contribution. Speak to members of professional organizations for computer experts or members of computer clubs to discover ways to teach computer skills. Drug awareness, social development, fitness both physical and mental, and peer group sharing are all areas in which dedicated volunteers can offer support. Remember to call upon community organizations to assist in implementing programs. Seek advice from local law enforcement officials, social welfare workers, health administrators, professionals in the areas of fitness and wellness, and members of organizations such as MADD or A.A. Check the appendix for national addresses for some of these groups. Use them!

If you are a volunteer with good organizational skills, possess creative problem-solving skills, and are willing to commit time and energy, who knows what new programs you will implement in your building!

RESOURCES

Calkins, Lucy McCormick. *The Art of Teaching Writing*. Portsmith, N.J.: Heinemann, 1986.

Curran, Mary. Co-coordinator, Volunteer-Supported Writing Programs, Johnson Elementary School, Cedar Rapids, Iowa.

Derr, Laura. Volunteer, Johnson Elementary School, Cedar Rapids, Iowa.

Hunter, Pamela. Volunteer, Grace Abbott Elementary School, Omaha, Nebr.

Junior Great Books, Great Books Foundation, 40 E. Huron, Chicago, Ill. 60611.

Frank, Marjorie. *If You're Trying to Teach Kids to Write, You've Gotta Have This Book!* Nashville, Tenn.: Incentive Publications, 1979.

Lyons, Bill. "The PDQ Method of Responding to Writing." *English Journal* (March 1981).

National Commission on Resources for Youth. *New Roles for Youth in the Schools and the Community*. New York: Citation Press, 1974.

Parents and Kids Put Writing First. Lexington, Mass.: D. C. Heath, 1987.

Picture Person Parade. Community Education and Services, Independent School District 281, Community Education Center, Robbinsdale, Minn.

Walshe, R. D. "What's Basic to Teaching Writing?" *English Journal* (December 1979).

14 Mother Goose Goes to School
Organizing Special Events

Special events fall into many categories: all-school academic events, school carnivals, national holiday observations, community service projects, traditional local celebrations, ethnic holidays, social awareness programs, or school projects inspired by designated national observances such as National Book Week. Whatever the purpose or the observance, we designate as a special event all classrooms in a building. Think of these as comparable to the Emmy-award category "Single Program or Miniseries." (You, of course, are working toward the nomination of Best Director of a Single Program or Miniseries or, perhaps, Best Supporting Player.)

READING CELEBRATIONS

National Book Week, celebrated each fall, and Library Week, each spring, are two perfect springboards for special events on reading. To spotlight the importance of reading in everybody's life, invite guest readers to the classroom to share their favorite children's books. Parents and other "everyday" volunteers may come dressed in costume to read aloud from their favorite children's classics—or "not-so" classics.

Invite community leaders as special guest readers. "Officer Friendly" is certainly a community leader to a third-grader, as are the mayor, the school board president, local judges, doctors, and business leaders. Area sports heroes would be a big hit reading a sports story—or for real impact, a soft, cuddly story or a story about being scared. Community theater groups or storytellers might be invited to perform to the entire school at an assembly. Local authors might come and share their work similarly or in small groups which might ask questions about writing. Ask every staff member to recommend a favorite childhood book and make up a recommended book list.

Incentives and rewards for children's reading should be an important part of the Book Week celebration. Some schools set goals—a million minutes of reading or 7,000 books read in one week, and display large graphs which are updated daily. Graphic displays of performance are great fun for the kids. Children might write the titles of the books they have read on tiger and zebra stripes or leopard and jaguar spots and animals decorated with these spots or stripes could be hung around the building. Likewise, cut-out bear paws, footprints, Indian feathers, and others could be signed and displayed. Use motifs pertinent to your school's mascot or some other theme.

One year our school built a balloon bookworm. For each book read a balloon was inflated. Balloons were collected in large, clear plastic garbage bags. The bags were tied together to make a "bookworm" that stretched around the ceiling of the building from front hall to cafeteria. Another year, each child who read at least one book — in other words, every child in the building — received a balloon. On Friday afternoon of book week, we had a massive balloon launch. Attached to each balloon was a poem about the children's reading efforts and a plea to anyone who found the balloon to write back to the child whose name appeared in the blank at the school's address. Letters and telephone calls were received from folks hundreds of miles away; one balloon recipient donated money to the library to buy books.

Volunteers support all of these efforts by assisting with planning, making displays, working collection points, inflating balloons, tabulating reading lists, listening to beginning readers, writing titles on spots, and other activities.

"Read and Feed" is another idea that can be incorporated into such a celebration. Students who read or are read to for fifteen minutes each day earn a small bag of popcorn to munch on while they're reading or listening. Lucky volunteers can assist in the popping process and those even luckier individuals — there's a sucker born every minute! — can help with clean-up.

To reward outstanding individual effort, students who reach certain reading goals can be recognized in a number of ways. Their names could be announced over the intercom each morning, displayed on a central bulletin board, or they could be given mimeographed bookmarks. As children reach higher goals, give them greater rewards. They could graduate to fancier bookmarks — construction paper of individual design made earlier by students, crocheted, needlepointed, laminated, cross-stitched, or felt markers made by volunteers. Set goals to be reached in gradients of ten or twenty-five and make allowances for age differences; perhaps early readers could count by books with special recognition goals beginning at ten, older children by pages read beginning at twenty-five for second- and third-graders, fifty for fourth- and fifth-graders and increasing by multiples of the first number.

Another fun event that ties into Book Week is a book exchange. Based on the concept of a giant trading market, each child brings used books to school. Each bag is marked with child's name and the number of books contributed. Books are gathered over a week or two period, then on trade day the books are laid out on the playground or cafeteria tables or the floor of the gym. Classes are then scheduled in half-hour intervals to come look at the books and make their choices. Each child gets to take out of the exchange as many books as he or she brought in — within limits. It is a good idea to set a limit of ten books for each child and to make clear to the parents that the books should be suitable children's books. Teachers and volunteers need to make sure extra books are donated so that every child takes home at least one book even if the child could not donate any. Extra books may be solicited from parents, local libraries, the IMC, garage sales, and so on. Volunteers, of course, are essential, to collect books, keep records, display books, supervise the selection process, and clean up afterward. This project is an excellent method of demonstrating the fun and value of books and reading.

MATH PROGRAMS

'Nough of reading, let's give 'rithmetic equal time. It is often the case that at certain times of the year, many or all classrooms in a building are involved in intense math study. Usually in early spring, children are beginning to test the math skills they've learned that year by suffering the wretched and fearsome *timed test*. We've all done them and there's no denying that memorizing math facts can be boring and taking timed tests can be quite intimidating. Perhaps as volunteers, we can lighten our children's load — and the teacher's, too; they, after all, carry the burden of being the bad guys here — by introducing an element of fun into this rite of passage. We have some suggestions for ways in which volunteers can *add* their efforts to *multiply* the effectiveness of the math curriculum.

As volunteers, we can support our school's math curriculum by becoming involved in a one-week, all-school concentrated focus on mastering math skills. Volunteers can support such a special event first by being part of the planning and organization of such an event. Naturally, since this kind of event is very dependent on class curriculum, chairperson for such a planning committee should probably be a staff member, and all teachers must be consulted, but volunteers can serve as valuable support and resource assistants.

Before the big week, volunteers can make posters to hang around the building to focus attention on and build up excitement about the event. Volunteers can also be responsible for writing notes to parents or announcements in newsletters explaining the plans. Volunteers can design and make prizes, badges, certificates, ribbons, and buttons to be awarded to students who demonstrate mastery. Go *all out* here. Make sure every child in the building takes home at least one award during the week. Volunteers can decorate bulletin boards creatively using numbers or math themes. To encourage number recognition for smaller children, volunteers can number objects in the building—every step in the stairwells, the ceiling tiles along a long hall, the doors along the hallway, the sidewalk squares in front of the building, the hopscotch courts on the playground, the tables and/or chairs in the cafeteria, and the desks in the first-grade rooms.

During the week, volunteers can support the project by tutoring children with flash cards, playing card games such as War and Cribbage, playing math games, grading timed tests, and checking skill sheets. Volunteers can also encourage measurement skills by working with groups of children in such projects as measuring distances. For example, children could measure a distance in the building using different units of measure and displaying results. A main bulletin board could graph the distance from the IMC to the cafeteria in feet, yards, meters, adult footsteps, child's steps. Groups could use crepe paper along the ceiling or wall to represent differing lengths—a blue strip is ten feet; yellow, three yards; green, three meters; and red, a mile; or an average car, a commercial jet, and an oil tanker; or the length of a tennis court, a football field, and a basketball court. A display case could illustrate a pound of somethings—nails, feathers, iron, aluminum, water, wood, flour, nuts, coffee, or candy.

The entire building could get involved in a project of counting to a million or even a thousand. Surely we've all heard of schools who have collected a million bottle caps. Volunteers can be the support system for such a project by helping children count and store the collected items. Collect a big number of anything recyclable and add an element of charity to your project by donating proceeds for the returns to the homeless or a local wildlife preserve. Collect a thousand pennies and donate the money to charity or school improvements.

DRUG AWARENESS

It is a sign of the times that drug awareness programs are a matter of course in elementary schools these days. Substance abuse education should begin in kindergarten and continue through elementary school and beyond. Volunteers can assist in this education effort by serving as organizers of special awareness events, locating and contacting resource organizations and individuals, and acting as supplementary work sources in preparing learning materials.

Usually local law enforcement agencies, police departments, and/or area substance abuse councils have combined forces to come up with drug awareness programs designed for elementary-aged children. The first step in planning any such special event concerning substance abuse should be to contact one or all of these organizations. As a volunteer, you may act as liaison between the school and these agencies; making contacts, organizing materials, scheduling speakers, and so on.

In the building, staff members such as the school nurse, the health secretary, the counselor, and the principal should all be excellent sources of resources, materials, and creative ideas about drug awareness programs. Since addressing the problem of drug abuse requires more than just educating the child about drugs and their side effects, activities involving building the child's self-concept, dealing with peer pressure, and following one's conscience must be part of any program.

Like the math or reading awareness weeks, a successful drug awareness week should teach important lessons but also be fun and involve the children in the learning process. Thus the building should be festooned with antidrug and/or self-awareness posters—designed by kids! Every person in the building could wear a "Just Say No" button or badge made by volunteers. All week every class could work on crossword puzzles, coloring pages and graphs, word finds, and resource work sheets all focusing on the drug theme, prepared by volunteers. Puppet shows or skits speaking to this issue could be presented to and/or by children. Children could write reports and stories about drugs or the effects of drug addiction or the difficulty of fighting peer pressure about drugs—or anything else.

Guest speakers might be an important part of such a drug awareness event. Bringing one in may be as simple as making a couple of telephone calls, or it may require a little digging and expertise. First, contact the community agencies mentioned above for information about such speakers. Police departments often have an "Officer Friendly" program in which an officer has been trained to speak to young ones about such issues and will come to your building free of charge. If there is no Officer Friendly program in your area, contact your nearest Sears, Roebuck store, the sponsors for Officer Friendly programs across the country. The same may be true of other agencies and/or hospitals or clinics dealing with drug problems. Alternatively, you may want to schedule one of the many speakers available locally or nationally through a speakers' bureau. This last possibility may require funding which you may have to seek outside your building. Principals and other staff may be the resources for finding out where to seek funds through the educational system, or volunteers may seek funds from private corporations or organizations. However funding is raised, volunteers can act as valuable resources in locating funds, making applications for such monies, begging from individuals or groups, and/or writing up proposals for funding.

As a postscript, let us add that the issues of street smarts (strangers, who they are and how to react to them, what to do in an emergency, how to be a latchkey kid) and self-protection and preservation (saying no to adults who want to touch private parts, dealing with abusive parents or other relatives, keeping dangerous secrets) are also part of the current curriculum at elementary schools. Such issues may be equally represented in another special awareness week, "Street Smarts and How to Get 'Em," during which activities similar to those outlined could be presented. Or drug awareness, street smarts, and self-preservation could all be lumped together in one special event week called "I Care about Me" or something similar.

ONE-DAY EVENTS

Make-it-and-Take-it Craft Day

A craft day is fun for kids and volunteers and a great way to allow the kids to experiment with arts and crafts projects that they wouldn't have time for in school. It is also a good opportunity for children to learn the very special lesson of handcrafting a gift for someone else, so such days could be scheduled before gift-giving holidays such as Hanukkah, Christmas, Mother's or Father's Day, and/or Valentine's Day. Such an event may be scheduled as after-school event for all those interested children who sign up or as in-school activity with small groups scheduled to work with a volunteer for a half-hour or hour at a time.

For suitable craft project ideas, consult teachers, area craft experts, and teacher's, women's, and craft magazines. Remember to keep it very, very simple and open to much individual expression. Limit materials needed to paper, glue, crayons, scissors, supervisors, and imaginations. Extras like lace, ribbon, beads to string or not, doilies, stickers, fabric scraps, fancy papers, wallpaper, and so on are great but should not be essential. Projects such as greeting cards, collages, wall hangings, and holiday decorations are perfect. The absolute necessity for such a project is many patient volunteer and staff hands to maintain crowd control and to ensure that every little person leaves with a project that they are proud to give.

Artists in the Schools

Several states around the country have arts councils through which it is possible to schedule special events revolving around local and regional artists. Artists come into elementary schools and lead presentations about their art, usually incorporating student participation. Such visitations may be variously scheduled: one-day special visits, partial-week workshops, or week-long events. A single building may wish to schedule all an artist's time or a group of schools may combine to share an artist's visit. Artists range from puppeteers to opera singers, from poets to folk artists. In Iowa artists are paid for their efforts with a combination of funds from the Iowa Arts Council and the individual school, either through school budgets or PTA funds. Investigate to find out if your state offers such a program. Your state arts council can then send you information listing the artists available, the funding required for the visits, and the steps required to secure such a program. There will be forms to fill out, funds to apply for, records to keep, and so on, so it is best that a patient, well-organized soul who is unintimidated by bureaucracy be in charge of scheduling such events.

Gift Sale

There is a national company that markets the concept of a children's gift bazaar in a complete package. Whether you use the company or sponsor your own sale, the idea is to organize n one place a variety of gifts ranging in price from twenty-five cents to five or ten dollars and give children the opportunity to shop privately for holiday gifts for their family members. Children come to the bazaar and spend their own money however they want. One little girl, for instance, came to a sale with envelopes marked for each family member. The child and her mother had budgeted a dollar for each sibling, two dollars for each parent and a dollar for the girl herself. The little girl ended up spending fifty cents each on her brothers, sisters, and dad, twenty-five cents for herself, and used the rest on the very special item she found for her mother!

Despite the obvious commercialism in ordering the package from the national company, we still think this is a clever, educational concept that could be great fun for both volunteers and children. Of course, organizing such a sale on your own could be a great deal of work unless you could find a specialty shop or gift supply house that could provide a variety of items with guaranteed return; the national company we refer to does that for you. Contact your PTA president for information about the package available from the promotional firm; we're sure every PTA president in the country gets one of their fliers.

Spirit Day

Spirit days are usually sponsored by the school administration and staff, but volunteers can lend their support in many ways. First, of course, if your building does not have a regularly scheduled day during which all staff and students wear school colors and attend a school assembly to sing school songs and applaud all student and school achievement during that month or report card period, suggest one. Responsibility for organizing and scheduling such a day rests with the principal, but volunteers can help by dressing as school mascot, making reward buttons, putting school stamp or sticker on generic certificates of achievement, typing, or printing names on certificates, writing class cheers or school song, and gathering records of achievement—good grades, perfect attendance, good citizenship, and outside-of-school achievement.

SOCIAL AWARENESS AND SERVICE PROJECTS

Another area that could involve the entire building in a special event is the sponsoring of social awareness and/or service projects. Adopting an animal at the local zoo or wildlife preservation, city clean-ups, food and toy collections for needy families, adopting a grandparent, tree plantings, are all excellent service projects in which elementary school children can become involved.

Volunteers can help by researching the availability, feasibility, necessity of such projects. Here's a good way to indulge your personal interests a bit. Bird watchers aware of an endangered species in your area? Sponsor an adopt a bird project. Environmentalists? Set up a field day at the nature center where children help pick up litter, build a campfire area, and learn the long-term effects of disposing of nonbiodegradable plastics. Social-service oriented? Arrange a campaign to salvage a run-down home for the local homeless to use: Enlist kids to raise funds, collect household items, paint walls, and so on.

Volunteers are needed to coordinate all such efforts, find resource speakers, publicize and build enthusiasm for the project, supervise field trips, count monies, keep track of contributions of food and other materials, distribute contributions, and generally serve as role models in volunteerism. Two of the greatest concepts we can teach our children is the value of giving, and our responsibility to each other as fellow citizens of this planet.

OTHER "UP WITH KIDS" IDEAS

Schools like to recognize students for any number of important events in their lives. One fun birthday recognition would be to have the birthday child pick a favorite book to read or have the principal read aloud over the intercom the morning of the child's birthday. Volunteers could help here by contacting each birthday child and scheduling the readings.

Volunteers might sponsor a monthly birthday luncheon for all the birthday boys, girls, and teachers. Here's a great way to make children feel really special and have the opportunity to spend time with others with whom they have little in common except a birthdate. It is also a fun way to get to know children in a relaxed, happy atmosphere. If space allows, let each birthday child choose a friend to join him or her at lunch. This makes everyone a little more comfortable and also makes the invited guest feel special, too.

Birthday people could meet in a special area of cafeteria or another part of building to have lunch together and share their communal cake. Volunteers can act as hostesses at such events, set pretty tables in bright paperware, bring fresh flowers for a centerpiece, hand out a small birthday prize to each participant (something on the order of the fifteen-dollar-a-gross prizes one orders for school carnivals), and bake a special birthday cake.

FUND-RAISERS

All of these projects require volunteer time in planning and executing; some of them require funds and/or equipment. Sometimes small funds and/or materials can be donated easily and happily by volunteers or other members of the school community. But some volunteer projects require significant amounts of materials or just plain cash. Volunteers are, after all, already donating time; must we ask them for their money as well? While writing out checks may be a viable, satisfying way for some parents to contribute to their child's school, it is not practical to expect to finance every project on the goodness of someone's heart and the size of someone's pocketbook. Clearly, in the world of school volunteering as in so many other good works, fund-raising is necessary.

Fund-raising comes in all varieties, colors, shades, and levels of commitment. PTAs and PTOs are pretty good resources, for they have had experience with fund-raisers and know what has worked for them in the past, what other schools have done traditionally and consider "their" territory, and what simply won't play in your section of Peoria.

One of the most popular fund-raisers is, of course, selling a product—candy bars, calendars, books, cookies, wrapping paper, poinsettias, holly, or greeting cards. Numerous companies would be happy to help you with such a project, some good and some not so good. Check with your Better Business Bureau and a PTA that has used that company before committing yourself.

Some things to consider before you choose to sell a product marketed by fund-raising companies are: Do you want your elementary school children selling door to door? Or at all? Are you going to ask parents to be sellers? If you do not mind children selling, what level of competitiveness do you want—class versus class, grade versus grade, or child versus child? Who gets prizes—individual sellers, classes, or the whole school? Are the prizes worth the effort and the competitiveness that vying for them engenders? How about the item to be sold – is it too heavy for little ones to carry door to door? Is it a product appropriate for children, for your area of the country, for the general ethnic background of the school population? Is the product of good quality? Does the item to be sold have any academic or social value to your students? (We favor school logo T-shirts, sweat suits, books, pencils, and notebooks over candy, for example.) What about the probability of breakage or spoilage? Is the cost reasonable? Consider the work involved and levels of competency required to be successful. How confusing is the order sheet? How difficult is the pricing? Do you prepay for merchandise or postpay for orders and merchandise in hand? Is the percentage of possible profit worth the effort?

There are other alternatives to nationally marketed fund-raising sales campaigns, bake sales are one time-tested example. Those directed toward the children – a quarter a cookie, ten cents for a bag of popcorn – are not barn busters, but they do raise funds. Those nickels and dimes do add up. A no-bake sale is great for all burned-out bakers out there. Let participants contribute the amount they would have spent baking for a sale and earn the money without the calories.

Book fairs are another good fund-raiser. The basic concept of a book fair is that the company or bookstore provides a supply of books to the school, school volunteers sell the books receiving a predetermined amount of profit plus perhaps a certain number of bonus books – depending on the number of total books sold – for the school library, and leftover books go back to the company. Depending on the system of purchase the book fair requires – sometimes the school has to keep an inventory of the books, sometimes they don't, sometimes you can order books not on hand, sometimes not, sometimes kids fill out forms provided by the book fair, sometimes parents and children just come and browse – a considerable volunteer commitment. There are national companies that sponsor book fairs, and there are probably local representatives of such in your geographic region. Check with the school principal or the PTA for more information. Locally, bookstores may also sponsor school book fairs. We favor book fairs as they not only make money, they also reinforce the concept that reading is valuable.

School Carnival

Would any discussion of school fund-raisers be complete without mentioning school carnivals? Carnivals are very popular school functions all over the country, although your school may call them ice cream socials or fairs or circuses. In fact, you may recognize the evolutionary process that our own school carnival went through.

About ten years ago our school sponsored an ice cream social. Everybody was invited to come to school, buy an ice cream cone, a cupcake, or piece of pie, and a drink or cup of coffee. The price was modest, the point to raise funds for the PTA while raising school spirit and parental contact with the school and each other.

Great; everybody liked it. But maybe, folks started saying, we could do it even better. How about some games in the gym to keep kids from getting bored and wild. So they rented games like ring toss and bean bag toss from the city recreation department.

The games turned out to be such a great success, they added more. Some bright pragmatic type got the idea to charge to play the games to cover the rental fee. Good thinking. They not only paid the rent; they made a profit. And so began the Johnson School Carnival, *the* social event in every Johnson Jaguar's calendar and a definite money-maker for the PTA.

Each individual family profits from the fun of spending an inexpensive evening eating hot dogs and cake, playing games, meeting friends, winning lottery treats like Coca-Cola visors and free plays at the local arcade. After three hours of nearly 1,000 people wandering about an overcrowded school in May, all sweating like lemonade glasses in July, the PTA rakes in the cash – to the tune of something like $3,500 last year! Here are some of the tips our PTA has learned about running a successful carnival.

One of the first innovations was Traci's idea – to focus the carnival around a theme. The theme adds a whole new dimension to planning such an event by lending a special focus to decorations and activities. One of the first themes was just the carnival or "circus" idea. Thus posters, decorations, and activities all centered on the circus theme. We added a face-painting booth where a parent dressed as a clown transformed little cheeks into clown faces. Another volunteer sold balloon animals. Workers at the games were asked to come in costume if they wished. A professional button maker was donated and we sold buttons with circus designs or let children design their own right there at the booth. One booth sold children the opportunity of making their own computer-generated banners: The kids chose the design and pushed the button, then watched while the printer made their sign. We were getting educational.

A designer hot dog dinner was added to the fun. The fair spread to classrooms where we held games of bingo, a little bake sale, and a cake walk. (Many of the cakes used in this booth were made by children in one of the classroom kitchens. Melinda's son happened to be one of those children helping to bake cakes. He also happened to be one of the three children who mistook a bag of plaster of paris for the sack of flour and thus dusted his cake pan.... Never mind — so we were a couple of cakes short that year!)

Next year's theme was a Country Fair — perfect for Iowa and the mid-1980s when everything went country! The dinner turned into a "chuck wagon" though the menu was unchanged from the year before. The bake sale became a country store that expanded into two classrooms and included handmade items donated by crafty parents and children. A very successful lottery was held for a beautiful handmade quilt. (Melinda's still peeved she didn't win that!) To ensure lots of winners in the lottery, other prizes were solicited from area merchants and an integral part of all future carnivals was born — the door prize. To add a little more advertising power to their contribution, the name of each donating merchant was written on an ear of corn and displayed on the front lobby wall.

The fair became so popular that it began to rival Walt Disney World during spring break. The lines were terrible. To solve the problem of having to wait for tickets, a couple of weeks before the fair, the PTA sent home special envelopes with every child. Parents could send money and purchase food, lottery, door-prize, and games tickets ahead of time. Volunteers took ticket orders and counted money each morning, then returned each child's envelope to the proper classroom with the tickets stapled inside.

The carnival date for the next year fell on the fifth of May. Cinco de Mayo came to Iowa and has stayed for four years. (PTA decided that theme was so successful, they would keep it until the fifth of May fell on the weekend, and then it's back to the drawing board.)

Piñatas and Mexican sombreros festoon the halls each April, and any student families taking Mexican vacations are given a small allowance with which to buy prizes. We sell these items and pesos at the marketplace. The chuck wagon gave way to the taco bar served out of la cocina. (In the weeks before the celebration, Mexican words are pasted everywhere in the building.) Instead of painting faces, we now apply wounds to veterans of the Alamo. The boys just love to come out of that room wrapped in miles of gauze and dripping "blood" from multiple wounds — disgusting, but profitable. In a make-it-and-take-it room, titled Hecho in Mejico, little ones make birds and flowers from bright construction paper, paint clay tiles, and string colorful beads. The whole school has enjoyed learning about this Mexican holiday and joining our southern neighbors in its celebration.

A special event can be as extravagant as an all-school carnival or as unimposing as Poet's Corner. It can raise funds or awareness or simply spirits. It may support the community or encourage academic achievement. It can involve as few as one volunteer or as many as a hundred. It can be as big or small as you want to make it. All it takes to make any day special is you!

15 Bigger Fish to Fry

All-District Programs

Sometimes an idea comes along that is so interesting or a program so successful that creators and/or organizers wish to spread the wealth and let other schools in the district take advantage of the terrific program. Sometimes there comes an idea for enrichment that is without question worthwhile, but the implementation is so complicated and detailed that it doesn't seem worth pursuing for just one school. In any of these cases, it is time to think beyond just your own building; it is time to take a look at the larger picture; it is time to plan a program directed toward whole-district participation.

We highly recommend that you be a veteran volunteer before you embark on such an ambitious project. You need to have had much experience working with committees, working with resistant elements, and dealing with the educational community, in general. Ideally, you should have had past experience in setting up programs in your building. Your volunteer experiences in the past should have established you with the educational community, provided you with a wide variety of contacts from which to draw assistance and information, and prepared you for the amount of preparation that such a project will take. Your experience in volunteering should also have given you training in diplomacy and patience, organization and planning, not to mention the ability to get everything done that needs to be done in any meeting in one hour or less.

Assuming you have such experience, your procedures for establishing an all-district program are basically the same as those we outlined for establishing an all-school program. It's just that now your vision is more far-reaching and your program must necessarily involve a great many more people both in the execution of your program and in benefiting from its enrichment.

Your first step in initiating an all-district program is the same as the first step in establishing any program: determine a need. Talk to your school board members, your district superintendent, your state legislators, or send for relevant literature from any of these sources. Read the local and statewide documents which outline the goals and objectives for their schools. Read also any books you can find examining our public school systems and where we seem to be failing our children. (In order to avoid getting a one-sided view of things, be sure to at least skim several.) Talk to your favorite teachers—and not just ones in your building. Talk to your principal and ask to be introduced to principals in other buildings. Send out district-wide questionnaires asking teachers and administrators for their evaluations of the district needs and how volunteer-supported programs might help.

After such investigation, you will discover several areas in which all the experts agree we are not meeting the educational needs of our children. This is usually due to lack of funds. We can't pay the staff to teach necessary courses; we don't have the building space to include these activities; we don't have the time in the school day to meet all these needs. Volunteers can fill in these gaps. In the areas of foreign language and foreign cultural appreciation, scientific stimulation, whole-language development, fine-arts appreciation, and higher-level thinking skills, volunteers can establish enrichment programs that can benefit whole districts of children.

Once you have established needs, you must then determine in which area your program will focus; which specific needs are you going to try to meet? Will the program you establish focus on just one area of instruction? Is it possible to devise a format into which you can plug a number of programs that will fulfill a number of needs? What kinds of needs seem to be most pressing? Which of the needs might a volunteer program most feasibly meet? Are there ongoing programs in individual schools that address these needs and can they be adapted to serve the entire district? All of these questions need to be answered, and not by you alone. You guessed it: It's committee time.

No all-district program can be established without input from many members of that district community. Since the program will cross school boundary lines, representatives from a number of schools should be included on the committee. These members should be veteran volunteers with a history of getting along well with other members of the educational community. But don't leave others out; business leaders and/or organization presidents may be some of your most valuable contributors to programs of this kind.

A committee of six to eight members with one very definite, but diplomatic leader should meet first to determine which need or needs will be the focus of the program. Brainstorming ways in which a variety of programs could meet any one need or several needs is a good way to begin. Let the communal creative juices flow, and do not be judgmental about any idea at first. Just let the ideas form freely. Ride the early wave of enthusiasm and assign areas of further study. Let each committee member take responsibility for fleshing out one or two promising ideas before the next meeting.

At the next meeting, the committee should be able to decide on one or two avenues of programming that seem to merit extensive research. At this point, it is good to remember to keep your plans simple and small. Although the program may be intended to meet the needs of a large number of students, it need not be elaborate and/or complicated—quite the opposite. If so many children and buildings are to be included in the project, then its execution needs to be simple and straightforward, easily communicated to a large number of volunteers. Upon completion of the planning stage, the idea project should clearly fill an obvious and immediate need and be dazzling in its simplicity.

There are numerous cases that we could use to illustrate how to establish a successful all-school program. Interestingly enough, several such programs that we know about were products of the creative minds and hard work of members of Junior League organizations across the country. In Virginia, the Junior League initiated the Art-in-a-Suitcase program; in Houston, Texas, the League sponsored drug prevention puppet shows, offered a children's theater presentation to 15,366 third-graders, and assisted in kindergarten screening; and in Cedar Rapids, one of the local League's most successful educational programs has been the so-called Enrichment Unit Project. A careful examination of the evolution of this particular program presents a clear idea of the process of establishing any kind of all-district program.

Organized originally to supplement elementary school curriculums for gifted and talented children, the enrichment project in Cedar Rapids quickly threw out the exclusivity factor and focused on designing a program that would provide enrichment for all elementary children. First a committee studied the needs and goals of the district, interviewed district administrators, and sent out surveys to teachers and administrators to focus on specific interest areas. After compiling this research, several areas of study were decided upon including Iowa history, math enrichment, health and nutrition, French, and writing—in this case, a publication unit, since the local paper showed considerable interest in supporting such a program.

So we can see that the developers did their homework. They studied district needs, sought much expert advice, and called upon members of the community for input and assistance. Their next step was to assign committees to research each area of study. Five or six people on each committee did extensive research into each topic and came up with creative approaches to communicating the information.

The next step in the process was for research committees to decide upon a format for the enrichment program. In this case, the program was set up to make week-long visits to each school and reach every child in the building. A station system enabled developers to process many children through several facets of a presentation. It was decided to set up several simultaneous programs from which each school could pick one unit per year. Each unit would be staffed by a core of six to eight volunteers who would go to the building, set up the stations, and following prewritten scripts present a body of information including visual aids, hands-on materials, work sheets, design projects, mental exercises, and physical displays to the entire building population over the course of one week of mornings.

Sound easy? Things just moving along logically and easily without a hitch? If you're nodding your head, you obviously haven't worked on a lot of committees. Sally Harms, our informant on the details of setting up this program in Cedar Rapids, is quick to point out that while setting up such an all-encompassing program such as this requires much input from many sources, too many voices are sometimes like too many cooks. Once the basic format was set up, then the real work of researching each topic, finding resources and materials, narrowing topic areas, writing scripts, and establishing materials began. And therein lay the rub. Suddenly everybody became experts and everybody thought what they wanted was absolutely essential to the success of the program. That great, free flow of ideas so beneficial in the early stages of planning suddenly had to end. And a lucky somebody had to get out the old blue pencil and start playing editor.

So don't be in a rush to complete this step. There will be endless details, all of which each advocate will think infinitely important. The ultimate leader of such planning—and there had better be one—needs to be practically a saint, or at least one of those rare and wonderful people who can listen to everyone, be emphatic, and always keep the ball rolling in the right direction.

The weeks have passed. You have determined a real and present need that is recognized by staff, administration, and the community at large. You have devised a program to meet that need. You have researched the subject area and gathered resources and materials. You have established a simple, straightforward, easily administered format for communicating the information to the children in an interesting, creative manner. Now all you have to do is talk the teachers and principals into going along with you.

Remember what we said about resistance in chapter 5, for you are going to run into a lot of it with a program like this. No matter how carefully you have devised it to work for varying levels of ability and development, to fit easily into the regular school day with a minimum of interruption to building routine, no matter how well you have trained all your volunteer staff, you will find teachers and administrators who just don't see how they can possibly fit this program—even though it appears to be a valuable and worthwhile concept—into their day. Sally Harms advises hiring a diplomat with the skills of Henry Kissinger to smile, nod appreciatively, and quietly barrel her way right into that building while making them all think it was their idea to invite her!

The point is, don't give up. By now many, many hours have gone into making this program work; you and your fellow volunteers cannot let a little resistance—or even a lot—get you down. To be successful, all-district programs must be used by more than just the open-minded, willing-to-try-anything buildings; they must be accepted by the less-than-enthusiastic buildings as well or die from lack of interest in a year. The first year will be the toughest. So, listen; hear the objections, the concerns. Expect them and accept them, no matter how trivial. Smile, nod your head, and walk right around every one of them with creative solutions and oceans of flexibility.

The Cedar Rapids Junior League established the concept of Enrichment Units in our schools eight years ago. In the first year, four different units were offered to all elementary schools and staffed entirely by League volunteers. The program is now staffed by a part-time district employee—the League paid her salary for the first three years of her employment—and offers ten separate units. Building volunteers are trained to staff whichever one of the units their school has chosen for presentation that year.

It is clear that this program, like all good volunteer programs, evolved thanks to strong community commitment, careful planning and execution, and a sincere concern for meeting educational needs of all the children across the district. While this particular program serves as an ideal model, it is by no means unique. Across the country volunteers are serving their schools in a wide variety of all-district programming.

In the Payson, Arizona, schools, for example, a special-interest group and the community school district are working together to make possible an interesting all-district program. Sixteen volunteers from the Ganto Amateur Radio Association will be teaching 140 sixth-grade boys and girls how to construct and build their own AM radios. Eileen Lawson, area volunteer coordinator writes us:

> With the assistance of the "ham radio" club, the students have been assembling, wiring, and soldering their own radios. The cost is only $3.50 per child and all the materials were furnished by the "Ham" club. It is the hope of the Amateur Radio Club that in the years to come, some of these students will reflect on this experience and choose the science and engineering fields for their life career and become "Amateur Radio Ambassadors of Goodwill."

If you are interested in investigating the possibilities of establishing an all-district program in your community, begin with a trip through the Yellow Pages of your telephone book. Contact groups and/or local chapters of national organizations with a history of sponsoring and/or supporting such programming, such as the Junior League. Contact local businesses and area divisions of national corporations for assistance; Sears, Roebuck, area law enforcement agencies, and city hospitals. Special-interest groups may be interested in cochairing a service project featuring their expertise, like the ham radio enthusiasts in Arizona. Senior citizen groups or homes may be looking for an avenue of stimulation and interest.

All you may need to do to start an all-district or any other volunteer project is to make a telephone call. That one call may be the spark that lights the candle that ends in George Bush's "thousand points of light" across your district, across the country. Volunteering in our schools is truly a partnership. It just may enable you to join hands with your school and your community.

Appendix A

National Resource Organizations

Adam Walsh Resource Center
3111 S. Dixie Hwy., Suite 244
W. Palm Beach, FL 33405

Association for Volunteer Administration
P.O. Box 4584
Boulder, CO 80306

Association of Junior Leagues
600 1st Ave.
New York, NY 10016

Boy Scouts of America
1325 Walnut Hill Lane
Irving, TX 75038

Campfire
4601 Madison Ave.
Kansas City, MO 64112

Girl Scouts, U.S.A.
830 3rd Ave. and 51st St.
New York, NY 10022

Jack and Jill of America
1065 Gordon St. SW
Atlanta, GA 30310

League of Women Voters of United States
1730 M St. NW
Washington, DC 20036

MADD, Mothers Against Drunk Drivers
669 Airport Hwy., Suite 310
Hurst, TX 76053

National Association of Elementary School Principals
1615 Duke St.
Alexandria, VA 22314

National Association of Partners in Education
601 Wythe St., Suite 200
Alexandria VA 22314

National Conference on Parent Involvement
579 W. Iroquois
Pontiac, MI 48053

National PTA
700 N. Rush St.
Chicago, IL 60611

Officer Friendly Program
Sears, Roebuck and Co.
Sears Tower
Chicago, IL 60604

Parents Anonymous
6733 Sepulveda, Suite 270
Los Angeles, CA 90045

Retired Citizen Volunteer Program
806 Connecticut Ave. NW, Rm. 1006
Washington, DC 20525

VOLUNTEERS: The National Center
111 N. 19th St., Suite 500
Arlington, VA 22209

YWCA
101 N. Wacker Dr.
Chicago, IL 60606

YWCA
726 Broadway
New York, NY 10003

Appendix B
Examples of Volunteer Handbooks and Materials

Dear School Volunteer,

This handbook has been prepared to offer volunteers specific information relating to duties and responsibilities of the volunteer at school. It cannot begin to contain all of the information necessary to meet your needs, but it is a beginning and background to help you feel comfortable in the very important task of helping to meet the needs of students and teachers.

District Volunteer Office

398-2124

VOLUNTEER
HANDBOOK

PARTNERS IN EDUCATION

Cedar Rapids Community Schools   Cedar Rapids, Iowa

GOALS OF THE VOLUNTEER PROGRAM....

The School Volunteer Program of the Cedar Rapids Community School District operates with the approval of the Board of Education and the School Administration, and is at all times guided by the principles and policies of the School District. Volunteers work in school under the direction of teachers or other professional personnel to strengthen the school program and/or offer special skills to enrich a student's educational experiences.

With students from many diverse backgrounds, each school has a personality of its own. However, the general aims of all Volunteer Programs shall be:

. To assist teachers in providing more individualization and enrichment of instruction for the students.

. To enrich the students' experiences beyond what is normally available in schools through the unique resources which can be contributed by volunteers and the community.

. To increase students' motivation for learning.

. To relieve teachers of certain non-teaching tasks and duties.

. To provide an opportunity for interested community members to participate effectively in a school's program.

. To strengthen school-community relations through positive participation.

. To build an understanding of school problems among citizens, thus stimulating widespread involvement in the total education process.

2

INTRODUCTION ....

Q. WHO IS A VOLUNTEER IN EDUCATION?

A. *A Volunteer in Education is a concerned and dedicated person who is not paid and works regularly, or as needed, in schools or other educational settings to support the efforts of professional personnel. The use of volunteers is restricted to those activities requested, approved, and supervised by a District employee.*

Teachers frequently wish they had more time to give to each student--to listen and to respond, to individualize instruction, and to meet the unique needs of each learner. School volunteers can help make this wish come true.

A volunteer is many things: an extra pair of hands, an extra measure of personal warmth, a valuable resource for classroom enrichment, a bridge between the instructional program and the community. We can't buy what volunteers give our schools.

No longer are school volunteers only parents; they are also grandparents, high school and college students, retirees, and business employees who get release time to serve in the classroom.

As a volunteer, you are assisting the staff in their day-to-day endeavor to provide the best possible educational experiences for each child in the school. So that you may be more effective, you may want to better understand your role, and how your task relates to the goals of the Cedar Rapids school system.

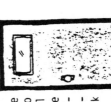

1

THE ROLE OF A VOLUNTEER . . .

Volunteers are assigned only upon the request of the teacher, principal, or other school personnel for volunteer service. Whenever possible volunteers are assigned where they wish to serve. They serve only in an auxiliary capacity under the direction and supervision of professional school personnel. A volunteer supplies supplemental and supportive service and is not a substitute for a member of the school staff.

A volunteer does not have access to confidential files and records.

The relationship between volunteers and the school staff should be one of mutual respect and confidence.

THE OUTSTANDING VOLUNTEER WILL . . .

Look at volunteering as a way to learn new skills, make new friends, and improve the community.

Maintain a sense of humor

As you work in the school, always maintain your sense of humor. People will love you for it!

Keep calm in emergencies

Know what to do and where to get help if it is needed.

Maintain a positive and professional attitude

Respect the confidentiality of all information and activities related to students and others in the school. Leave the responsibility for diagnosis, prescription and evaluation of students to teachers. Be willing and able to comply with school rules.

3

VOLUNTEER PROCEDURES AND RESPONSIBILITIES . . .

ARRIVAL

Be sure to wear your nametag when you volunteer. It provides identification for staff members, other adults, and students.

A time sheet will be posted in the school's Volunteer Center for you to use each time you volunteer. This will enable us to keep a record of the amount of time you have given. The building coordinator is responsible for maintaining information on the sign-in sheet and submitting a monthly log sheet to the District Office. Help your coordinator by recording your hours!

DEPENDABILITY (KEEP YOUR COMMITMENT!)

The staff you work with will depend upon YOU to be present at your scheduled time. Their tasks are planned with your help in mind. If you will not be able to volunteer on a particular day, please notify at once the school office and leave a message for the staff. (No-shows are frustrating for both teachers and eager students.)

CONFIDENTIALITY

Please remember! All of your work is confidential. Names of pupils, teachers, and staff, their actions and abilities are never appropriate topics for discussion outside of school.

4

INSURANCE FOR VOLUNTEERS...

The following information is intended to clarify insurance coverage provided by the School District for volunteers serving in the Cedar Rapids Community Schools. Each section describes the insurance coverage that volunteers possess under the District's Workers' Compensation, General Liability and Motor Vehicle insurance policies.

SUMMARY OF COVERAGES

1. Workers' Compensation Insurance

Volunteers injured on the job while performing duties for the District are covered under the District's Workers' Compensation insurance. This coverage would pay medical and/or hospital bills for injuries sustained according to the Iowa Workers' Compensation statutes in carrying out duties as a Volunteer worker for the District.

If the volunteer is injured while on the way to school or on the way home from school, there is no coverage available under the Workers' Compensation insurance. This exclusion also applies to all regular paid employees of the District.

2. General Liability Insurance

Volunteers are covered by the District's Comprehensive General Liability insurance provided the volunteer is acting within the scope of his/her authority. This coverage includes the District's Basic Liability policy and the Excess Umbrella Liability policy. Volunteers are covered by this policy while performing various assigned volunteer duties such as school office work, supervisory duties during playground activities or field trips and other similar authorized duties. This same coverage applies to all employees of the District.

6

TIPS...

. Attend training/orientation sessions as offered.

. Express a genuine interest in helping students.

. Call the students by name at each opportunity.

. Observe closely the techniques used by the teacher and try to model these instructional methods when working with individual students.

. Give assistance when asked, but try not to supply answers before the student has a chance to solve the problem on his/her own.

. Listen attentively; encourage and praise students for even the smallest success.

. Let students know you recognize their efforts when they are behaving well.

. Leave the technical job of teaching to the teacher.

. Inform the teacher if a behavior problem arises. The teacher will want to carry out the classroom and school discipline plan.

5

Insurance Coverage cont'd

3. Motor Vehicle Insurance

Volunteers should be aware of the limitation of insurance coverage while driving motor vehicles for school purposes such as a field trip. If the volunteer is driving a school-owned vehicle, the driver is covered by the District's Motor Vehicle insurance and the Excess Umbrella insurance policy.

If the volunteer is driving his/her own or a family-owned vehicle for purposes such as a field trip, the volunteer is liable for his/her own liability coverage. The District's Motor Vehicle insurance does not cover the volunteer's personal motor vehicle. Volunteers should make certain that their personal motor vehicle insurance provides adequate liability coverage. The District cannot purchase insurance coverage for a volunteer's personal motor vehicle.

Furthur questions concerning the District's insurance coverage should be directed to the District's Business Office located at 346 Second Avenue S.W., Cedar Rapids, Iowa 52404.

7

Tulsa Public Schools

SCHOOL VOLUNTEERS

... VOLUNTEER ...

_____Yes, I want to be a FROST SCIENCE CENTER VOLUNTEER

NAME_____PHONE_____

ADDRESS_____ZIP_____

CHILD'S NAME_____GRADE_____

I am interested in working in the following areas:

_____ Reading - listening to children read, creative writing, supervising games

_____ Science - one-to-one tutoring, special projects and experiments

_____ Math   - one-to-one tutoring, flash cards

_____ Plan Parties

_____ Field Trips - plan, make necessary arrangements, chaperone

_____ Clerical - at home _____ at school _____

_____ Great Books Discussion Leader - lead small group discussion, specialized
                                      training available.

I am available to volunteer on:

    Monday___   Tuesday___   Wednesday___   Thursday___   Friday___

        Mornings_____   Afternoons_____   Full Day_____

Please return to the Business/Community Resources office, P.O. Box 45208, Tulsa,
OK, 74147.

                            WELCOME ABOARD!!!

                                    Nancy McDonald
                                    Director
                                    Business/Community Resources

Approved: Dr. Jack Griffin

SHOW OF INTEREST
Volunteer Information Sheet

If you are interested in possibly becoming a school volunteer, please fill out
the following:

Name _____   Telephone number _____

Address _____

Child's name _____   Classroom _____

Best time to contact you _____

I am possibly interested in volunteering in the following area(s):

    <u>At School</u>   ____ Kindergarten
                    ____ Other grade level (i.e. 1st, 2nd grade, L.D.)
                            specify _____
                    ____ IMC
                    ____ Clerical

    <u>Field Trips</u>   ____ Supervisor

    <u>At Home</u>   ____ Typing
                    ____ Preparing games/bulletin board materials
                            (Teacher provides all instructions and materials)

    <u>Enrichment Unit</u>   ____ (Special, portable, one week activity that build-
                            ing sign up for - French, Publications, etc.)

I am possibly available to volunteer:

    ____ once a week   ____ twice a month   ____ other (specify)
    ____ occasionally for enrichment activities   _____

Personal Inventory

I am: ____ an idea person   ____ a craft person   ____ a stickler for details

         ____ an organizer   ____ good with machines   ____ good with children

         ____ activity oriented   ____ musically inclined

         ____ other _____

Occupation _____

Hobbies (please be specific) _____

I am willing: ____ to share my occupation or hobbies with students at this school.

               ____ to be entered in the School District Resource file and share my
                    occupation or hobbies at other schools.

Thanks for your cooperation!

PATCHOGUE-MEDFORD PUBLIC SCHOOLS
APPLICATION FOR VOLUNTEER SERVICE
241 South Ocean Avenue
Patchogue, New York 11772
(516) 758-1000

Name _____ Date_____

Address_____ Town_____ Zip_____

Telephone Number (Home)_____ (Office)_____

In case of emergency, contact:_____ Telephone Number_____

Patchogue-Medford Residents Only:

<u>Names of Children Attending School</u>   <u>Grade and School Attending</u>

_____

_____

_____

EDUCATION

_____

	<u>Name & Location</u>	<u>Dates Attended</u>	<u>Degree</u>

<u>High School</u>_____

Post High
<u>School</u>_____

_____

In what capacity would you like to volunteer?

1) Speakers' Bureau_____
(list subject or field of expertise)

2) Tutor_____ Level_____ Subject_____

3) Tutor (Special Education)_____ Level_____

4) General Classroom Assistant_____ Level_____

5) Student Tutor_____ Level_____ Present Grade_____

6) Clerical (Office)_____ Level_____

7) Clerical (Classroom)_____ Level_____

8) English as a Second Language (specify language)_____

PATCHOGUE-MEDFORD PUBLIC SCHOOLS
OFFICE OF SCHOOL VOLUNTEER PROGRAMS
241 South Ocean Avenue
Patchogue, New York 11772
(516) 758-1000, Extension 312

SCHOOL VOLUNTEER REFERENCE REQUEST

Please return by_____

Re:_____

1. How long have you known this person?_____

2. In what capacity do you know this person?

   relative _____   co-worker _____

   friend _____   neighbor _____

   employer _____   other _____ (i.e., civic organizations. Please specify)

3. Describe the applicant's personal characteristics, abilities, and talents which you feel makes this individual suitable to work with students:

   _____

   _____

4. Describe your knowledge of any volunteer activities in which the applicant has been involved:_____

   _____

   _____

5. Provide any information which you feel might minimize the applicant's contributions to the Patchogue-Medford School Volunteer Program:_____

   _____

   _____

6. Provide additional information which may assist the Patchogue-Medford School District in considering the applicant for volunteer service:_____

   _____

   _____

   _____

   _____

_____   _____
        Date   Signature

                                _____
                                Please print/type name

IMPORTANT

1. All qualified applicants will receive consideration without regard to age, race, color, religion, marital status, sex, national origin, military status, or handicaps.

2. If appointed, additional data may be required for statistical purposes.

3. The use of this application does not indicate there are volunteer positions open and does not in any way obligate the school district.

"THE PATCHOGUE-MEDFORD SCHOOL DISTRICT IS AN EQUAL OPPORTUNITY EMPLOYER"

TULSA PUBLIC SCHOOLS
SCHOOL VOLUNTEER PROGRAM

VOLUNTEER-TEACHER ORIENTATION/CONFERENCE CHECKLIST

Teacher's Name _____

Volunteer's Name _____ Date of Conference _____

Check after discussion with volunteer:

_____ 1. Identification of child (children) to be tutored (pertinent
background information)

_____ 2. The special needs of the child

_____ 3. The special strengths of the child

_____ 4. How the volunteer can best help in the overall instructional plan
for the child (i.e. curriculum areas)

_____ 5. Tutoring tips which can be helpful with the specific child
(i.e. reinforcement techniques, evaluative procedure)

_____ 6. Particular materials, strategies, or games which can be utilized

_____ 7. Time and days of tutoring

_____ 8. Procedure for summoning child (i.e. entrance and exit guidelines)

_____ 9. Designation of work area location

_____ 10. Procedure for volunteer and teacher to keep in touch (i.e. regular
conferences, informal meetings, telephone conversations)

_____ 11. Discussion of classroom and school rules and emergency procedures

_____ 12. Designation of alternative plans if assigned tutee or teacher is
absent

_____ 13. What progress has been made by the child

_____ 14. What additional skills need to be developed and practiced

_____ 15. What, if any, difficulties have been encountered in volunteer's
efforts with the child

_____ 16. Expression of appreciation of volunteer's service

TULSA PUBLIC SCHOOLS
SCHOOL VOLUNTEER PROGRAM

TEACHER/SCHOOL VOLUNTEER PLANNING SHEET

NAME OF VOLUNTEER _____

NAME OF TEACHER _____ GRADE LEVEL _____

NAME(S) OF STUDENT(S) _____

_____

_____

SKILLS TO BE REINFORCED OR TASK TO BE COMPLETED

_____

_____

_____

_____

TIME BLOCK _____

MATERIALS TO BE USED _____

_____

_____

_____

LOCATION OF MATERIALS _____

_____

PROCEDURES _____

_____

_____

COMMENTS BY VOLUNTEER

_____

_____

_____

_____

FOR MOST EFFICIENT USE, KEEP IN A FOLDER FOR VOLUNTEERS

TULSA PUBLIC SCHOOLS
SCHOOL VOLUNTEER PROGRAM

TEACHER-SCHOOL VOLUNTEER AGREEMENT FOR VOLUNTEER SERVICES

Date _____

Teacher _____

School Volunteer _____

Day(s) School Volunteer will serve _____ Time(s) _____

1. Specific volunteer duties agreed to by teacher and volunteer:

   _____

   _____

   _____

   _____

   _____

   _____

   _____

   _____

2. Training required and when it will be given: _____

   _____

   _____

3. What to do if volunteer needs help: _____

   _____

4. Where volunteer will work. (Ex.: in library, in classroom, elsewhere)

   _____

5. If volunteer works with students in a group, what is the maximum number of
   student with whom this volunteer wishes to work at one time: _____

   _____

The teacher and volunteer should feel free to change their minds if the
arrangements need adaptation. Duties, therefore, should be re-evaluated
by teacher and volunteer 4-6 weeks after volunteer begins services.

25 Ways to Show Appreciation to Your Volunteer
(choose those which are appropriate to your situation)

1. Greet the volunteer by name; encourage students to use volunteer's name.

2. Try to thank the volunteer personally each day, noting special contributions.

3. Set a time to talk with the volunteer when children are not present; speak briefly with the volunteer each day before departure.

4. Celebrate the volunteer's birthday, and encourage students to write occasional thank-you notes.

5. Use the volunteer's special talents, knowledge and interests in assigning tasks.

6. Give the volunteer increasing responsibilities and more challenging tasks.

7. Share articles and books of mutual interest--on child development, learning styles, or content area in which the volunteer works.

8. Include the volunteer when planning class activities.

9. Include the volunteer in staff meetings and inservice training when appropriate.

10. Send a letter of appreciation.

11. Take the volunteer to lunch.

12. Call or write when the volunteer is absent or ill.

13. Invite experienced volunteers to train newer volunteers.

14. Ask the volunteer coordinator about training which might appeal to the volunteer; can the PTA offer a scholarship so volunteer can attend conference or workshop?

15. Write an article on the volunteer's contributions for your volunteer newsletter, school newspaper, or community paper.

16. Ask the volunteer coordinator or school community relations staff person about a feature story on volunteers for the newspaper, radio, or TV station.

17. Nominate your volunteer for a volunteer award.

18. Celebrate outstanding contributions or achievements.

19. Commend the volunteer to supervisory staff.

20. Ask volunteers to help evaluate program and suggest improvements.

21. Help plan a recognition event--an assembly, reception, or luncheon; invite the superintendent, school board, administrators, parents, and community leaders.

22. Ask the children to evaluate the performance of volunteers; share their comments with the volunteers.

23. Accommodate the volunteer's personal needs and problems.

24. Enable the volunteer to grow on the job.

25. Write a letter of recommendation when the volunteer requests it.

*from NSVP "Effective Involvement of School Volunteers"

(SUGGESTED) CALENDAR FOR BUILDING COORDINATOR

AUGUST

Teacher Inservice days

* Meet with principal
* Contact former volunteers
  -letter/telephone
* Attend District meeting for building coordinators

DISTRICT VOLUNTEER OFFICE
* Community Awareness Effort
* Building Volunteer Coordinator Meeting
* Contact local colleges to determine number of student volunteer participants
* Recruit Kindergarten Screeners

SEPTEMBER

* Survey teacher needs
* Activate core group
* Contact former volunteers/ meet early needs
* Prepare volunteer center
* Recruit new volunteers
  -letter/telephone
* PTA Open House
  -distribute brochures
* Plan Building Orientation Session
  -former vol. participate
  -principal participates
  -register new volunteers
* Schedule all volunteers
* Turn in monthly log sheet by the 5th of the month

DISTRICT VOLUNTEER OFFICE
* Community Awareness Effort
* Attend Building Orientations
* Plan Vol. Skills Workshops
* Recruit Kindergarten Screeners

OCTOBER

* Complete scheduling of all volunteers
* Up-date Information Due; send to District Office
  -vol. names, addresses for mailing list
  -community resource possibilities
* Encourage vol. to attend Skills Workshops, Governor's Conference
* Volunteer Ventilation: "How is it going?"
* Send monthly log sheet to District Office by the 5th

DISTRICT VOLUNTEER OFFICE
* Volunteer Skills Workshops
* Enrichment Units
* District Volunteer Newsletter, "The Volunteer Connection"

NOVEMBER

* Teacher Ventilation: "How is it going?"
* Informal evaluation and Recognition
  -thank you notes from students
  -(Thanksgiving)
  -coffee
  -item in school newsletter
* Observe and maintain program
* Send monthly log sheet to the District Office by the 5th of the month

DISTRICT VOLUNTEER OFFICE
* Coordinator Ventilation: "How is it going?"
* Enrichment Units

DECEMBER

* Recruit new coordinator, if appropriate (Principal and coordinator)
* Send monthly log sheet to the District by the 5th of the month
* Enjoy Winter Break!

DISTRICT VOLUNTEER OFFICE
* Enrichment Units
* Enjoy Winter Break!

JANUARY

* Coordinator year begins (applicable to some buildings)
  -meet with principal to review plans
* Survey staff needs for second semester
* Recruit to meet new needs
  -telephone
  -letter (with report cards)
* Up-date records; notify District Office
* Attend District meeting for building coordinators
* Send monthly log sheet to District Office by the 5th of the month

DISTRICT VOLUNTEER OFFICE
* Community Awareness Effort
* District Volunteer Newsletter
* Enrichment Units
* Meeting for building coordinators

FEBRUARY

* Orientation for new volunteers at building level, if needed
* Schedule new volunteers
* Up-date Information Due- send to District Volunteer Office
* Send monthly log sheet to District Office by 5th of the month

DISTRICT VOLUNTEER OFFICE
* District Meeting of Building Volunteer Coordinators
* Place Field Experience Students
* Enrichment Units

MARCH

* Special Awareness of Volunteer Activities
  -posters
  -item in school newsletter
* Send monthly log sheet to the District Office by the 5th of the month

DISTRICT VOLUNTEER OFFICE
* City-wide meeting for volunteers (focus and date to be announced)
* Enrichment Units

APRIL

* Volunteer Recognition
  -certificates (available from District Office)
  -thank you notes
  -tea/appreciation luncheon
* Awareness-Kindergarten Round-up
  -bulletin board
  -brochures
* Send monthly log sheet to the District Office by 5th of the month

DISTRICT VOLUNTEER OFFICE
* Public Awareness - Bulletin Board Displays
* Recruit K-Screeners
* Enrichment Units
* Coordinator Recognition

MAY

* Evaluation of program (available from District office)
* Thank you notes
* Meet with principal/ District Office
  -identify new coordinator
  -review year
  -project for fall
* Send log sheet to District Office by the 5th of the month
* Send end of year hours in as soon as possible

DISTRICT VOLUNTEER OFFICE
* Enrichment Units
* Contact new coordinators if known
* Yearly report

EVALUATION OF SCHOOL VOLUNTEER PROGRAM

<u>Principal's Annual Evaluation</u>

SCHOOL _____(Optional)_____ Principal _____(Optional)_____

Please fill out the following questionnaire to help us evaluate the School
Volunteer Program. Please answer candidly. Your opinions, judgments, and
suggestions are needed and will be used to improve next year's volunteer program.

1. Has the general reaction of the staff to the School Volunteers been:
    Good _____ Fair _____ Poor _____.

2. How many on your staff worked with volunteers? _____

3. Has the liaison between you and the School Volunteer Coordinator in your
    school been satisfactory? _____

4. Has the liaison between you and the District Office been satisfactory?___

5. Has the help given to individual children or small groups of children
    tended to improve their achievement level? _____
    (If you have statistics or specific examples, please attach)

6. Were there any problems in connection with volunteers? _____
    If so, what were they? _____
    _____

7. Has the on-the-job training of volunteers been satisfactory? _____

8. Do you believe the program is worthwhile? _____

9. Did this service make a contribution to the students in your school?_____

10. Would you like to have the School Volunteer Service continued at your
    school next year? _____

11. What kinds of service would you like to have? _____
    _____
    _____

12. Would you help the Office of School Volunteers with the following:
    a) Recruiting volunteers from your immediate community   Yes ___ No ___

    b) Orienting your staff on the effective utilization of
       volunteers   Yes ___ No ___

    c) Orienting volunteers to your school policies   Yes ___ No ___

13. Were you satisfied with the orientation received by volunteers in regard to:
    a) Volunteer commitment   Yes ___ No ___

    b) Volunteer attitude   Yes ___ No ___

    c) Volunteer relationship to children   Yes ___ No ___

    d) Volunteer relationship to staff   Yes ___ No ___

EVALUATION OF SCHOOL VOLUNTEER PROGRAM
TULSA PUBLIC SCHOOLS

<u>School Volunteer's Evaluation</u>

Please fill out the following questionnaire to help us evaluate the School Volunteer Program. Please answer candidly. Your opinions, judgments, and suggestions are needed and will be used to improve next year's volunteer program.

1. What was your job as a School Volunteer? _____
_____

2. Did you enjoy working as a School Volunteer? Yes ___ No ___

3. Of all the duties assigned to you, which did you enjoy the most? _____
_____

4. Which did you enjoy the least? _____

5. If tutoring, did you notice any improvement in the student's performance during your sessions? Behavior? _____ Attendance? _____
Grades _____ For specific cases use back of form.

6. Did you find the people with whom you worked willing to give you guidance and direction? _____

7. Did the orientation meetings for volunteers give you most of the information you needed before you started to work? _____

8. If you received any training, did you feel it was:
Adequate _____ Unnecessary _____ Insufficient _____

9. How did the children react to you as a volunteer? _____
_____

10. Did the faculty and staff seem to appreciate your efforts? _____

11. Did you have a sense of accomplishment in the job you were performing?
_____

12. Do you feel this program is worthwhile? _____

13. Do you wish to serve as a volunteer during the next school year? _____
If so, would you like to stay in the same school? _____
Would you like to stay in the same area of service? _____

14. Do you feel the contact with your School Coordinator was:
Adequate _____ Too frequent _____ Insufficient _____

14. Have the procedures for assigning volunteers to schools been satisfactory?
_____
_____

15. Does your school have as many volunteers as needed? _____

16. Was there evidence that the use of volunteers improved school-community
relations? _____
_____

17. Do you have suggestions on how volunteer service can be improved? (Please
feel free to indicate these.) _____
_____
_____
_____

Thank you for your assistance. Please return form to:

        Nancy McDonald
        Director
        Business/Community Resources
        Tulsa Public Schools

VOLUNTEER SELF-EVALUATION FORM

HOW AM I DOING ? ? ?

1. Do I plan for the activity which I have been assigned to, not hit and miss or just doing something?

2. Do I make myself helpful by offering my services to the teacher when there is an obvious need for help?

3. Do I have a plan for getting children into groups?

4. Do I observe closely so as to know children's or adult's likes, dislikes, preferences, enthusiasms, aversions, etc.?

5. Do I find opportunities for giving students choices or do I tell them what to do?

6. Have I given some individual help in writing?

7. Do I observe closely the techniques used by the teacher, and follow through when I am working with the group?

8. Do I emphasize the times when students behave well and minimize the times when they fail to do so?

9. Do I really listen to what students have to say?

10. Do I evaluate myself at intervals?

11. Do I accept criticisms and suggestions without becoming emotionally upset?

12. Do I follow directions of the teacher?

13. Do I try to develop a friendly attitude with all of my co-workers?

14. Do I give the teacher adequate notice of absences by reporting them to the office before the day begins?

15. Do I realize that my whole purpose for being in the classroom is to assist the teacher in order that the students might progress more rapidly?

16. Do I give too much help to students rather than allowing them time to think?

17. Do I refrain from interfering between another teacher and student unless called upon for assistance?

18. Do I avoid criticism of the student, teacher, and the school or agency?

(This self-evaluation form can be used at any point during a program. It can be used to suggest areas in which joint volunteer-professional training is needed.)

VOLUNTEER QUESTIONNAIRE

The following questionnaire is to serve as a tool for building coordinators to review the School Volunteer Program and to make improvements.

Please complete the following form. To make the School Volunteer Program even better, we need YOUR opinion.

1. What was the most enjoyable experience/s for you as a volunteer?

2. What changes or improvements do you suggest that will help the Volunteer Program next year?

3. What was the most frustrating aspect of your volunteer service?

4. List a few of the duties that you performed this past year.

5. Would you like to work as a volunteer next year?

   In the same capacity?_____

   In a different capacity?_____

NAME _____

DATE _____

Please return to Building Volunteer Coordinator

TEACHER QUESTIONNAIRE

The following questionnaire is to serve as a tool for te   _ers to review the School Volunteer Program and to make improvements

Please complete the following form.   ᴛ ᵤ ke the School Volunteer Program even better, we need YOUR opinion.

1. What were the most outstanding benefits you and your students received from your volunteer's services?

2. What was the most frustrating aspect/s in your utilization of volunteers?

3. What changes or improvements do you suggest that will help the Volunteer Program next year?

4. Would you like to have a volunteer next year?

NAME _____

GRADE _____

Please return to Building Volunteer Coordinator

EVALUATION OF SCHOOL VOLUNTEER PROGRAM

Teacher's Annual Evaluation

Please fill out the following questionnaire to help us evaluate the School Volunteer program. Please answer candidly. Your opinions, judgments, and suggestions are needed and will be used to improve next year's volunteer program.

SCHOOL _____ TEACHER _____

(or other staff member)

GRADE _____ (Signing name is optional)

1. Did the volunteers assigned to your class perform satisfactorily?_____
   _____

2. Were they willing to work under the direction of the teachers and
   principal? _____

3. Do you feel the School Volunteer was given adequate training before she/he
   was assigned? _____

4. Has the on-the-job training of the volunteer proved satisfactory? _____
   _____

5. Were your volunteers regular in attendance? _____

6. Has the reaction of the children to the volunteer been
   Good _____
   Satisfactory _____
   Poor _____

7. Would you like to have a School Volunteer assigned to you next year?
   Regularly _____ Occasionally _____ Never _____

8. Was the time spent in your room per week by the volunteers adequate? ___
   _____

9. Would you like more orientation or information on what to expect of the
   volunteer or what is expected of you? _____

10. Was your working relationship with the School Volunteer Coordinator
    satisfactory? _____ If not, why?
    _____

11. In what respects is the School Volunteer Program achieving the most *
    success? _____
    _____

12. In what respects is the Volunteer Program in greatest need of
    improvement? _____
    _____

Community Resource Volunteer Program:

1. Have you seen a copy of the "Career Education Speaker's Bureau"? _____

2. If you have used this program, has it been helpful? _____

   NOTE: If you have any additional comments, please feel free to indicate
   these on the back of form.

Thank you for your assistance. Please return form via school mail to:

Nancy McDonald
Director
Business/Community Resources
Tulsa Public Schools

Bibliography

ABC's: A Handbook for Educational Volunteers. Washington Technical Institute, 400 Connecticut Ave., NW, Washington, D.C.

Altbach, Philip G., Kelly, Gail P., and Weis, Lois. *Excellence in Education.* Buffalo, N.Y.: Prometheus Books, 1985.

Artists in the Schools. Des Moines, Iowa: Iowa Arts Council, Department of Cultural Affairs, Capitol Complex.

Bennet, Linda Leveque. *Volunteers in the School Media Center.* Englewood, Colo.: Libraries Unlimited, 1974.

Carter, Barbara, and Dapper, Gloria. *Organizing School Volunteer Programs.* New York: Citation Press, 1972.

Carter, Barbara, and Dapper, Gloria. *School Volunteers: What They Do and How They Do It.* New York: Citation Press, 1972.

Effective Involvement of School Volunteers: Handbook for Teachers. Alexandria, Va.: National School Volunteer Program, Inc.

Feeney, Helen M., and Stenzel, Anne K. *Volunteer Training and Development: A Manual for Community Groups.* New York: Seabury Press, 1968.

Frith, Terry. *Secrets Parents Should Know about Public Schools.* New York: Simon and Schuster, 1985.

Grandparents Coffee Handbook. Tulsa, Okla.: Tulsa Public Schools.

Hart, Leslie A. *Guide to School Change.* New Rochelle, N.Y.: Brian Age Publishers, 1982.

Janowitz, Gayle. *Helping Hands—Volunteer Work in Education.* Chicago, Ill.: University of Chicago Press, 1965.

Kappelman, Murray, and Ackerman, Paul. *Between Parent and School.* New York: Dial Press/James Wade, 1977.

Lippitt, Ronald, and Schindler-Rainman, Eva. *The Volunteer Community.* Fairfax, Va.: NTL Learning Resources Corporation, 1971, 1975.

McDonald, Nancy, and Zenke, Larry. *A Handbook for School Volunteers.* Tulsa, Okla.: Tulsa Public Schools, Education Service Center, 1988.

Membership Directory. Alexandria, Va.: National School Volunteer Program, Inc., 1988.

A Nation at Risk. Washington, D.C.: National Commission on Excellence in Education, April 1983.

National Commission on Resources for Youth. *New Roles for Youth in the School and the Community.* New York: Citation Press, 1974.

Picture Person Parade. Community Education and Services, Independent School District 281, Community Education Center, Robbinsdale, Minn.

School Volunteer Manual. Patchogue, N.Y.: Patchogue-Medford Schools.

Trecker, Audrey R., and Harleigh, B. *Handbook of Community Service Projects.* New York: Association Press, 1960.

VIPS Annual Report. Houston, Tex.: Houston Independent School District, 1988.

VIPS, Volunteers in Public Schools Handbook. Houston, Tex.: Houston Independent School District, 1988.

VIPS, Volunteers in Public Schools. Milwaukee, Wis.: Milwaukee Public Schools.

Volunteer Coordinator's Handbook. Cedar Rapids, Iowa: Cedar Rapids Community Schools.

Volunteer Handbook. Cedar Rapids, Iowa: Cedar Rapids Community Schools.

Volunteer Handbook. Duval, Fla.: Duval County Schools.

Working Together, District Eleven School Volunteer Handbook. Colorado Springs, Colo.: Colorado Springs Public Schools.

Index